Breaking Into SAP MM

SAP MM Interview Questions
(Second Edition)
SAP MM Certification

Jordan Schliem & Jim Stewart

EQUITY PRESS

SAP MM Certification Questions, Answers, and Explanations: 2nd Edition

ISBN: 978-1-60332-095-5

Printed in the United States of America

Please visit our website at www.sapcookbook.com

TABLE OF CONTENTS

PART I: WELCOME TO SAP

Chapter One

Welcome

Welcome to *Breaking Into SAP MM*. I'm really excited about this series, and I hope you get as much out of this book as I did writing it. There are far too many formal books out there that distance the reader with difficult language, and I didn't want this book to be like books that end up unread, unutilized, and in the trash bin. Please think of this book as an open conversation between you and me.

In this book, I cover everything you need to know to be a success, from how to prepare your resume to how to talk to recruiters. I'll discuss how to get your foot into the door in SAP, and then I'll show you how to move from a permanent employee to a consultant to a contractor.

Nature of Employment

The first important thing to discuss is the nature of employment in information technology. Some questions you may have are: What are the types of employment? What career paths are available? Is information technology a profession?

One thing is for sure, information technology is a culture of hard work, so be prepared.

The best way to talk about information technology careers is through aggression tactics and how people typically move through their careers. It's important to look at the ways that people work. The basic argument here is the status of the employee: are you a permanent employee or a contractor?

Here's an example:

General Mills is a very large food producer in America. So if you're a permanent employee and you work for them, they pay payroll taxes for you, etc. It's very simple to understand. You work for General Mills.

On the other hand, there are contractors. A contractor is an independent person. Many times, they work for a contracting firm, or they incorporate themselves. The contacting firm typically takes a percentage of their contractor's earnings. As an independent contractor, you don't have any employment taxes withheld and you're responsible for taking care of your tax needs and bookkeeping.

The last group of people in this mix is consultants. There's a fine line between a contractor and a consultant, but in general, the term "consultant" can be used to refer to anyone in information technology. This works in a general way, but a little precision never hurts. It is best to think in terms of questions like: Are you permanent? Are you contractor? Are you a consultant?

Consultants are permanent employees working on the behalf of big, multinational consulting companies. One very typical career path is to start working as a permanent employee at a large, famous company. Once you've learned enough, then you can go work as a consultant. When you're working as a consultant, you can work with several different clients rather than just one.

If you're working as a permanent employee for an automobile parts manufacturer, you learn one set of business processes and one set of rules. You learn one bureaucracy. This is as an example of a permanent employee.

One of the reasons consultants are so successful at what they do is that they have the ability to move between companies. For example, a consultant can go to five businesses and learn how five businesses work. They would have learned five computer systems or five SAP implementations. So in many ways you might say, "Well, the consultant is five times more valuable than the permanent employee because that's what work in today's global economy is all about: how quickly you learn, how quickly you are able to adapt to situations you encounter, how well you are at adjusting to change, how good you are at adjusting to change."

If you make this kind of observation, you are definitely on the right track. Consultants learn very quickly what's going on, how to navigate the political landscape of an organization, what changes they can recommend to make a company better or make the software implementation run more smoothly. One of the career paths that I recommend, if you are serious about a future in SAP, is to get a job as a permanent employee for a company that runs SAP, so that you can one day become a consultant.

Once you've gained enough experience, then you'll apply to large consultancy firms. When you go to work as a consultant, your mission is to engage as many different clients as possible at the highest level that you can. You will need to focus in on what sort of assignments you should take. Are you technical? Are you a programmer? Are you a Basis person or are you a functional resource? In general, technical and functional career paths are very good options. Functional career paths are closer to management, so they are often perceived as being more important. Moving from a permanent employee to a consultant is certainly one of the great established career paths.

One of the key features of this kind of job is that there is no formal apprenticeship program to becoming a consultant. You just have to jump in and say, "Yep, I know it, let's go!" or "I'm already an expert." Starting off as a permanent employee might address that apprenticeship problem. You will also need to convince a hiring manager at a big company that you're smart enough and well trained enough to learn the software and do a competent job.

This section is titled Nature of Employment for good reason. It is absolutely pivotal that you know that there are permanent employees, consultants, and contractors. You need to know that each of these roles plays and fulfills an absolutely dynamic role in the landscape of work. If you don't understand it, then you aren't going know where you fit in, and it's just not going to work out very well for you.

So far, this chapter has discussed permanent employees and consultants. The next category of employee is contractor. Contractors are a special case of employment in SAP. I've been a contractor for most of my career because it's the most highly compensated of all the positions. Contractors are typically expected to hit the ground running. When you start, you are immediately adding value to the situation. You know exactly what you're doing and exactly where to go. Contractors are typically the most senior of all the people you'll encounter.

I think contracting rates in SAP, certainly for functional SAP people, shouldn't be very much below $150 an hour, in addition to expenses.

Finishing off that train of thought, one very common career progression is to start as a permanent employee for a couple of years. Then go to work as a consultant until you have contacts in the business. You know when the modules are hot. You know how to operate, and once you really get to know your stuff, then you go work as a contractor.

Now that I've set the stage for permanent employee, consultant, and contractor, it is important to discuss the dynamics inside an organization. There are significant things that you need to know about each of these different positions. Permanent employees are typically seen as very important people within the organization. If you're a consultant or contractor, your job in SAP is to make these people feel that you're teaching them something. There is definite job security here, and permanent employees have a big say in office politics. If you're a contractor, your job is to educate these people, to help support their positions when they take on implementations, and in return, they'll keep sending you jobs. It's the same for a consultant and a contractor. Your job is to help make permanent employee's lives easier and to teach them what they need to know.

All the positions in information technologies need each other. Sometimes there is adversity between the positions, and this just gets in the way of getting the job done. The best companies have addressed this, at a minimum, and have done a good enough job of making sure that employees don't feel threatened when a consultant or contactor is brought in.

The role of the consultant or contractor is to learn what's going on, understand the problem, solve the problem, help the client work through it, get the software installed, and then move on.

Contracting and consulting are very different. You want to learn as much as possible because many times, there's a position in management at the end of a contract. This can be very lucrative.

In conclusion, there are three work roles: permanent, contractor and consultants. Later in this book, I'll go into more detail about each position, but right now it is enough just to have a handle on the basics.

Choosing a Module

It's time to talk about deciding on your SAP focus. It should go without saying that your goal is to get a job from an employer with a live SAP implementation. Here, and each step of the way, you need a single-minded focus about what you want to do. I get a lot of questions from people saying, "Well, which module should I learn? I want to learn MM, SD, LE, and CRM, and that's going to be my focus." Well, what you need to do is choose and specialize in one area.

One of the things that I find in SAP training is that there are plenty of courses that cost 1,500 euro and will train you to be proficient in MM, SD, FICO, Basis, or CRM, but I haven't seen anything that tells you how to choose a module.

As a quick guide to help you decide on your focus, you have Basis. Basis includes the entire technical infrastructure, installing SAP onto a server, installing the servers themselves, and networking. If you have a background in technology, servers, and especially UNIX or NT, or if you want to work with operating systems, then you should pursue Basis training.

Basis happens to be a very hot area, so if you have any technical expertise or even an inclination to learn how to be technical, Basis is the best choice for you. A sub-area of Basis is Security. This covers adding users, creating login profiles, creating profiles about which users can use which applications, and how to partition access between the modules. For technical people, I recommend specializing in either Basis or Security.

The other modules are Materials Management, Sales and Distribution, Finance and Controlling, and Human Resources. There is also Customer Relationship Management and Supplier Relationship Management, which are for people that have been in the SAP business for 3–5 years. I suggest choosing MM, SD, FICO, or HR. If you have experience in sales or marketing or maybe in real estate, you might want to choose SD (Sales and Distribution).

SD and MM can provide long-term success and long-term stability in SAP consulting because they are two of the core modules. So MM, SD, HR, and FICO are four hot topics right now; choose one of these four modules unless you have technical expertise, want to be a programmer, or a Basis person.

What more is there to say about this in general? Breaking into SAP means getting your first job in SAP, and this book will show you ways to break into it. Your first focus is to get a job at a company that runs SAP. Decide on which module you will be your specialty, and then prepare your resume and yourself accordingly.

The preparation that you need to do is to convince an employer that you have something to offer. And if you don't have extensive experience in SAP, you need to bring something else to the table.

One way to get a job is to talk about other skills you have that can help in tricky situations. For example, you could say, "Hey, I'm a UNIX expert or I'm an NT expert or I'm a computer whiz. I can learn anything very quickly, and I promise that when I come to work for you, I'll dedicate all my focus and I'll get the job done for you. I'll learn SAP, and it's not a problem." Even better, in that interview, you say, "I've done this before. I have." If you don't have professional experience doing this, you say, "Well, I have my own SAP system at home. I've installed this ten different times. I know exactly what's required, and I have no problem – when I come to work for you, I'll have no problem doing it for you." See, that's a compelling argument to an employer.

So breaking into SAP means getting your foot in the door and getting that first job in SAP implementation by leveraging experience you already have.

One of the core fundamentals is work to learn. Think about your job applications with that in mind. If you're applying for an SD job, you come to the table with experience in sales and experience configuring SD. Later in this book, I'll show you how to get experience before you have your interview. You will have a narrative of what you bring to the table, how you can help your employer, and in return, you're going to have certain criteria for what they're going to give you.

Are they going to let you configure the system? Are they going to send you to training? You should have a very specific idea of what your employer is going to bring to the table, as well as what they're going to offer you as an employee. You always want to take jobs with the future in mind. Some questions to ask: are they going to implement any other modules? What modules are already implemented? For example, if you get a job in SD, are they running CRM?

So you're very interested in getting into CRM. "I want to work for a company that has a live CRM implementation." That sounds good to an employer because it shows you're interested in your future and in learning about SAP. It is always good to demonstrate curiosity in an interview.

So we're talking about deciding what to learn. This is your first step. You need to decide what interests you. Using some of the techniques I'll tell you about later, you'll learn everything you can do before actually getting a job. You're going to do some preparation work. Then you'll start interviewing, and then you'll land a job. So, we're talking about three steps. Decide what you want to do, learn as much as possible, and start interviewing.

During the interview process, you're going to fail at some point, but that's fine. During the course of your interviewing, you'll ask your interviewer, "What do you think? Is there anything else you're looking for? What could I do better?" You should remember all the questions they ask you so you'll be that much better prepared for the next interview.

This especially applies to people in the rich west like the UK, Australia, Europe, and the United States. You're going to face a lot of competition from emerging markets in terms of programming, and therefore, I recommend that even if you're a programmer, to focus on Basis or Security (i.e. things that require much more of your physical presence at a job site). So that is the official SAP Cookbook recommendation. If you're technical, go for Basis or Security; if your expertise is solely with programming, choose Basis.

These areas are also very hot right now, and you might want to examine the demand for these. The demand for programmers is decreasing, for many reasons. SAP is a Commercial Off-The-Shelf (COTS) package. Companies are implementing the standard SAP solution more and more, and there's a greater demand for functional people over programmers. So, why torture yourself? Don't start off on the wrong foot.

There are plenty of rewards, too, if you can get started in Basis. These include some of the highest earning rates, some of the best jobs, and some of the easiest jobs (no offense to the Basis people). Yet, you want to think about your future, too. The highest paid people in IT are applications people, project managers, and they don't typically come out of the technical area.

Choose one. Choose only one area. Some people go their whole careers focusing on even subareas of MM. For example, I know a guy who's an MM purchasing expert. That's all he does. Don't feel like you have to learn everything. You can have quite a successful career in just one area. You can't even know it all, really, in one particular module in SAP.

To wrap this up: again, your first step today is deciding what area of SAP will be your specialty. The next step is preparing all the resources and materials that you need for the interview. The third is landing the interview and going through the interview process until you finally get that first job. Once you get that first job in SAP, you're on your way to a successful career as an SAP consultant or a contractor.

Module Prep

This chapter is the real core of this book, in my opinion. I have five steps about how to prepare yourself for a module. Questions this chapter will answer include: What do you do if you want to become an MM consultant, FICO consultant into HR, etc.?

If you follow the steps outlined in this section, I believe that you can acquire the skills and knowledge to succeed in your interviews. These are the steps I would follow if I wanted to learn something new. Everybody is always learning something new, and if you're not, well, prepare to be unemployed. Learning how to learn is a vital skill.

I am not going to speak specifically to MM or SD or HR or to any other module. Instead, I'm going to give you general guidance for what you need to do to learn. The first step is to gain access to an SAP system, especially with live system access. Obviously, if you want to learn something, you go ahead and do it and start practicing.

I know this might seem obvious to some people, but you can purchase access to a live SAP system. In fact it comes with our "Breaking into SAP" product. You should be getting notes via email or online that will point you to the way, but you also need to subscribe to IDES Access or another provider of SAP remote access. It allows you to log on to an SAP system, ECC5, ECC6, and start exploring and start working in the module.

Now, let me run through the five steps just briefly. I believe you can acquire the necessary skills by obtaining access to a live SAP system, which is step number one. Number two is to purchase every book on your module or your area of interest. Really, just buy everything. Third, go to http://help.sap.com/ and print out everything that SAP has on the selected module.

When I prepare for modules, I use three or four binders to hold print outs of all the information on the module. You will need it all eventually. Number four, print out all the configuration notes and the configuration details. After you have access to your system and go into transaction SPRO, you'll see a little notebook icon to the left of the configuration. Go to each configuration step in your area. Print those out and include them in your binders, as well.

Number five, take all these resources that you have and use these to walk through every configuration step for your module, execute every important transaction, and create the appropriate documents that comprise the outcome of your module system.

I think having everything really gives you confidence. Let's say that after you read everything, you still think, "Well, maybe I still don't know this." However, you will then know how everybody else feels, too. There will be some holes and gaps in your knowledge, and those gaps will only be filled in by working in SAP. You'll learn more as you use and configure the system.

So step one is getting access to the system. Step two: you've got all the books. Now you're going to start step three: using these books, getting on the system, starting to experiment, and going through all the configurations.

You're reading all your books and everything you printed out everything on http://help.sap.com/, which will take some time, and now you're starting to get the big picture and an understanding of how this fits in. You understand the transactions, how the documents move and interact, and the relationship between all of the different transactions in your module.

You're using these now to go into the system and walk through every single configuration step, even if you don't understand it. Go to every important transaction and go to every important screen in your area and create these documents. Try to understand the relationship. Your goal is to learn the module so well that you can explain exactly what it does.

You need to describe the relationship between the documents. You need to understand and explain to somebody on a philosophical, high-level basis, what this module does for a company, how it can help them, how it can drive efficiency, and how it can save them money. You need to be able to explain the configuration artifacts and the scenarios that might not be clear to you. You need to explain interactions with the org plan.

I firmly believe that it's a good idea to understand the frequently asked questions and troubleshooting with the module. If you go to http://www.sapcookbook.com, you'll see we've published dozens of FAQ books. And I think if you understand what we do, if you understand http://www.sapcookbook.com, then you understand that these books represent the most common problems people experience.

It's an incredible advantage for you to be able to say (especially in your interview): "Okay. Well, you know, what I always find to be the key risks or the key problems with SRM are approvals and transferring the org plan." That's why these interview question books are so effective. They help you understand the questions people are asking. And by reading the questions people are asking, it'll inspire you to think and to understand the software in a way that I believe is very effective and can help you land a job.

You can follow the basic roadmap of this chapter throughout your career. You'll want to maintain access to an SAP system. You'll want to have all the books available. You'll want to print out all the http://help.sap.com/ Help documentation. You'll want to print out all the config notes, and you want to gather their resources to walk through all the configurations, execute every transaction, and create every document.

The outcome is that you will be able to explain or describe what it is a particular module does, its purpose, and how it drives efficiencies in a company. You'll want to do that in an end-to-end manner, starting with how the users get started or what kicks off this process, what initiates the business process, and all the way to the outcomes of the order printing out to the printer. You need to be able to speak about the specific steps you took to configure the system, what artifacts in the configuration need to be changed, the scenarios, and the work plan. You also need to know the common problems with the module.

Here's an example:

Let me tell you about SRM. I don't know if you'd consider it a module in SAP, but it's an active consulting area. Supplier Relationship Manager (SRM) in SAP helps companies understand where they spend their money. Organizational spending is divided into indirect spending and direct spending.

Indirect spending has to do with pencils and papers, things that are incidental, but not involved directly in the product itself. For example, if we were selling cars, the sheet metal required to build the body is a direct cost or a direct expense; whereas the computers that we use in the office to design these cars is an indirect cost. Therefore, SRM further divides direct and indirect costs into commodities.

It's a good idea when you're using commodities to use an UNSPSC code, which is a standard code for different commodities such as paper or pencil, electronics. So what can you do when an SRM system is properly implemented? You can use it to drive efficiencies in spending and understand where your company is spending money. And the only way to drive efficiency in spending is if you understand where your costs are and can use understanding to leverage better deals with your vendors.

If you're spending $1 million with each of ten different vendors, maybe you can funnel back spending to just two of the vendors and drive better. What's the best way to save money in business? Drive volume. SRM also provides e-sourcing, standard workflows for approval processes, RFX and bidding, and auctioning. These are the most common ways SRM is used in an organization.

The documents, you start with a shopping cart, a shopping cart moves to approvals. Depending on your scenario, you can purchase requisitions or purchase orders created in the system. Purchase orders are printed and either faxed manually. They can also be sent via EDI in an XML format.

You're going to learn how to do that with your module, to give a five minute talk about what the module does, its function, how it drives efficiencies, and the documents.

These five steps are pivotal: getting access, getting the books, printing the help, printing the config, and then learning the module. If you can do this, you can repeat it for learning any number of modules.

Do I Know Enough?

How much knowledge is enough to qualify to land a job working in SAP?

It is important to first know that the vast majority of learning SAP is done on the job. You will always have the resources at hand to look up the answers that you need to do your job, and it's understood that you may not have everything memorized. If you are presented with a zinger and freeze up or act really nervous, this can cause people to raise their eyebrows and question if you know what you're doing.

The answer to "Do I Know Enough?" is really another question. Do you feel like you have enough confidence to talk about your module? Do you feel like you have enough confidence to give a 5-10 minute explanation of what your module does and how it helps a business become more efficient? Can you describe how to install the module, what the major risks are, and/or what the major pain points are for installing the module?

If you can explain to me what your module does and what the problems with the configuration are, then it sounds pretty good during an interview. Most people faced with a clear explanation will say, "Let's bring this person on because this gets back to what the interviewing process is all about." It is important to be well prepared for interviews because the interview is the door you need to get through in order to get the job.

Many other classes might emphasize that you need to know everything or you need a certain amount of knowledge before you can get started. However, I really believe that if you can pass an interview, you will learn everything on the job. Frankly, not a lot of people will tell you this secret: you don't need to know a whole lot to be successful. You just need to know enough to pass the interview, and once you get the job, that's where your learning is done.

So do you know enough? You're probably asking yourself this question right now. The answer is: Do you feel confident enough to talk about the module, what it does, how it works, and how to configure it? If the answer is yes, then you know enough.

Actually, it can actually be detrimental if you know too much. No one likes a know-it-all. A company would rather have somebody who has a more balanced approach to their knowledge. Of course it's nice if they have helpful input and they know their stuff. This is great, but you also don't want it to be taken to the extreme.

One way to think about this is: do you know where to go to get the right answers? The people who can do this are the most successful and enjoyable to be around. An excellent way to cover this in an interview is to say, "I learn every day, and I think an important part of me as a worker is that I always know how to find the right answer or I have access to a demo system, and if something doesn't work in one of your systems, I can try it elsewhere." Being a resource person is a good thing. Knowing where to go to get the answer is only OK.

You don't have to know everything. It's okay to have some gaps in your knowledge. The real question is: Do you have the confidence to fix a problem on the fly, or do you have the confidence to know who to call to get the right answer? Do you have the confidence to go to a forum, post your question, and get an answer?

I think you want to err on the side of confidence. If somebody states with confidence and authority an answer to an interview question, the interviewer might give that person the benefit of the doubt even if the interviewee was slightly off or gave an incomplete answer. Being assertive, and knowing how to speak effectively and with confidence, goes a long way.

Developing that confidence also prepares you to answer questions you may not know the answer to. If somebody hits you with a question that you don't have the answer for, or maybe don't even know where to start, you can learn and practice thinking about this and how to respond. In this situation, I would say, "Rather than giving you exact right answer, I would prefer to take this question offline and take a few moments to make sure I have the correct answer. I've run into this before and I know where to find the answer for this. I just want to write down the scenario you're asking me about and I will make sure that I find the right answer for you." Very few people are going to respond negatively to that kind of an answer.

Most of the time, you do have an answer. After all, you do need to be one or two steps ahead of your client in terms of knowing and anticipating the questions they're going to ask. If you don't understand something, speak up right away. Part of being an IT professional is finding information you need.

If you follow this book and look at the resources I provide, you will probably know enough. You may not think you do, but when you arrive at your project and realize that everybody else has the same worries that you do, you'll feel a lot better.

There might be a couple of guys like me in the room, but hopefully they'll extend enough professional courtesy to not hit you with a zinger. Everybody doesn't have a dozen or more years of experience working with these problems, and the fact is that people with all ranges of experience are needed on projects, and people with good attitudes are nice to work with.

As you're preparing, remember that. In your interview, try to come off as likeable and as friendly as possible. You'd rather work with somebody that you'd be friends with than somebody who just has an attitude. Nobody likes to work with somebody unpleasant.

Chapter Two

Experience

What criteria does a prospective employer use to evaluate you?

Your education, credentials, certifications, and classes you've taken are the primary considerations. What do you need to send an employer? Your resume needs your education, experience, academic awards, things that you've done. It is also needs your personal information on it, so be careful about how you present yourself. Your email address, your phone number, and your name should all be audience appropriate. For example, you should create an email address that has SAP in it. It's a simple thing, but people miss out on that first very easy opportunity to show your involvement in SAP.

To return to the larger topic of experience. The reason it's so important in IT is because there really is no other measure; only recently are there any university programs for studying information technology. There certainly aren't any programs studying in SAP. SAP is software. So just understand that employers can't really look at your education and know as much about you; whereas in other fields, a person's education says everything about their training. SAP just isn't like most other skills.

Another important thing is certifications. Certifications have historically not been as popular in the United States as elsewhere in the world. Some certifications might be worth more than others, but all in all, I think that certificates will not be considered a huge perk to your resume. A certification is "nice to have".

However, I think even the soft skills, and how well you interview, will trump certifications. All things being equal, if you have two people with the same level of certifications, experience will be the decisive factor. I'm not telling you that experience is the only thing that matters, or that certifications don't matter. Why employers think certification is important is because it's an indicator that you have done something in the past. And in the employment market, all that counts is: have you done this before? In an area like SAP, where things are very detailed, experience is pivotal. For example, every time I interview, I am asked whether I have configured SRM in the extended classic scenario with automated PO. Having done this before gives me an edge.

When you interview, you need to draw on your strengths. For example, if you went through a computer programming education, you know how to write computer programs. Another thing you learn as a programming student is how to use methods like divide and conquer to break up problems. This tells me that you can write programs, you can solve problems, and you know how to think in a certain way. And if you've done that, then I know that you're absolutely 100% qualified to install any module of SAP and do it with excellence.

Regardless of your experience, I think it's important for you to say that you've done it before; otherwise, they you won't get hired. It's a personal choice. It's totally up to you, but I'll just put it out there. In the global IT job market, the only way to get a job is to say that you've done it before.

When somebody asks me if I have configured something in a particular way and I say, "No, I haven't done that before, but I can easily do it," it just doesn't work. When you say, "Yeah, I can do this. I've done it before," even if you haven't, it gives them the reassurance that you know what you're doing and that you can come on without any problems.

For me, I can say I've done it before because I know that I can solve any problem in IT. I also know that I can solve any problem in SAP, so I feel justified in telling them that. They're going to ask you if you've done it before, and if they don't know any better or don't know the right questions to ask, they'll just ask: "Have you done it before?"

They may ask you, "Have you done it before?" because they don't know what else to ask you. It's really hard to ask somebody a question that will completely reveal their knowledge and understanding of a particular area, so interviewers tend to fumble a bit.

I hope it's clear that more than anything else, experience is what an employer looks for. It's the easiest indicator that you know how to do something, that you've done it before, even if doing it before isn't that important. You know, that's why it's the key factor in a resume. Of course, there are exceptions. Some people can look at a resume and really read the details. For example, if I saw your resume and saw you had a computer science degree from a research university and that you were working in some managerial capacity, I would still say, "Yeah, this is no problem. This person is fine." If you luck out and have an interviewer like me, then they won't ask you so many detailed experience questions.

Experience is the only indicator most of the interviewers have to go on, and it's an inaccurate practice at best. It only really helps them to make a guess about your abilities.

If you've only been studying SAP for a year and the job requires six years, well, I'll leave it to you to decide what to put on your resume, knowing what I've said, mainly that you won't get the job unless you have a competitive number of years experience and unless you say that you've done it before. I don't think anybody else out there is going to tell you that, but that's just how it is.

Ethical Considerations for Interviews

I think computer programming and information technology is a trade, and I say that because there's no formal apprenticeship that one must go through to become an IT professional. In reality, there are no beginners. There certainly aren't any jobs, or if there are, they are very, very few and far between for beginner SAP people.

So how does one get started with SAP? The first way I'll discuss is a method I learned from my friend Mike. He's an industry veteran of 25 years, so when he wants to break into a new area of technology, he gets a job as a project manager. Since he has 25 years of experience, he can easily get the project manager job, and I think that's excellent. But does that apply to everybody? How many people can claim 25 years experience? The most important things are how quickly you learn and how you treat your clients. My point here is that one strategy is to get a non-technical job in project management (if you have many years of experience) and take a job in the area of technology you're interested in.

One the other hand, if you are like me when I started out, you don't have any experience in SAP. However, I did have some useful skills. I was a UNIX systems programmer. I could install software. I could write shell scripts. I had technical skills to bring to the table for a company that had an SAP implementation. I was lucky enough to get a steady job as a UNIX systems programmer, where I was also trained in SAP.

It was a very satisfactory position to be in because I was utilizing skills that I had in exchange for SAP training. This is an example of junior-level applicants with skills that a hiring manager will find attractive.

The last category is for people who have no practical SAP experience and/or no SAP work experience. How does someone in this category break into SAP? It's important to understand the market that you're working in. I received a resume from somebody the other day claiming to have 12 years of experience in SRM. The catch is that SRM has only been around for 4-5 years, so I was very surprised. This is impossible.

The first thing to say about that tactic is that any experienced manager, any expert certainly, would look at that and say, "Oh, that's ridiculous and they can't have this many years of experience," and they would delete the email and would never hire the person.

Now as we know, not everybody is an expert, so they'll look at this resume with 12 years experience and they'll say, "Wonderful, 12 years. Okay, let's schedule an interview with this individual." Whereas when commenting on a resume with six years experience, which is a fantastic amount of experience by the way, they might say, "This person nets half the amount of time."

How do you answer these kinds of questions in your resume? As an example, on my resume you'll see things like Microsoft Word, Excel, PowerPoint, Access, Oracle, and UNIX. Now I have not been engaged as a full-time Microsoft Word expert for the last ten years, but it's still on my resume. And by that same token, I have not consistently used Microsoft Access over the last ten years, but it's on my resume. I also have SAP BW on my resume as well as MM. I haven't been working in these areas, either, but let me tell you what I have done: I have installed the BW software from scratch. I have used the Becks Analyzer.

It seems like I'm making justifications for exaggerating on your resume, but in this case, I don't think it's exaggerating, and I don't think it's unethical. The market for IT talent is imperfect and is driven by acronyms, letters and numbers on your resume that nobody understands, not even the hiring managers. And so if the right letters and numbers aren't on the resume, you won't get in the door or have the opportunity to sell yourself further.

Before I move on, I think it needs to be said that your resume must include all of the skill sets for the job you're trying to land. If you're going for an SRM Version 5.5 with Seuss, that needs to be there, and you need to say that you have experience working with that. You'll put it on your resume under the last place you worked, and you'll go get that experience and figure out just what it is that you need to do. And do not apply for a job with some experience that you don't have and don't know how to obtain or don't feel comfortable with; it will be a very bad outcome. Know your limitations.

You have some room here. I don't think it's unethical to put these things on your resume. In fact, I think it's necessary. It's an increasingly competitive market, and you need to change how you think and understand the reality. If you don't have the experience on your resume, you will never get the job. If you do have it on your resume, you may get the call, you may get an interview, and you may get a chance to prove that you are the person they want to hire. And when you get that job, it's time to perform and learn what you need to learn to get the job done. The real skill in IT is learning quickly and knowing how to solve your company's problems.

SAP INTERVIEW QUESTIONS

In conclusion, the resume is, at best, an imperfect mechanism for communicating your experiences. Many people have taken advantage of the imperfection, and it's an individual question for what to include and what to exclude. Remember: if your resume says that you don't have the needed experience, you will be passed by.

It's necessary to learn what you need to learn. You assume that there is some sort of continuity in the products, and you brush up your resume with clever jobs. It can be quite controversial, but I think in today's market, you're justified putting things on your resume if you're confident that you can execute them once you're at work.

Interview Question Books

If you are familiar with SAP COOKBOOK, you'll know we are the premier publisher of interview question books in SAP. I am the owner and publisher of Equity Press and http://www.sapcookbook.com. We started in 2005, when I published a book about SRM called *The SRM Advanced EBP Cookbook*. After selling a couple hundred copies, I thought the cookbook was very focused and very oriented in helping people do the configuration. If you look at this book, it tells you step-by-step how to do configurations, but it doesn't address anything about really doing the work in SRM, and it certainly didn't address getting a job in SRM or in SAP generally.

The product of this line of thought was interview question books that have three parts: a table of contents, content, and an index. These books do not tell you how to do the work once you're at your client. They don't tell you how to get the job done.

These interview questions books are condensed down to only the most important kernels of information that you need to understand to get a job. Some people are very doubtful of this kind of book and think that the amount of information you would need to know could never be contained in a single book. In fact, all you do need to know to get the job is contained in this book. This brings us back to a previous discussion: the dilemma about what to say in an interview, what to put in a resume, and whether you're confident enough to fulfill the duties in SAP PM. If you buy this book and can interview successfully after having used it, you are halfway there.

Interview books, and what they represent, are a reflection of where information technology is today and where it's going in the future. I think the tools are getting better, the technology is getting better, the business processes are better documented, and they're generalized. I think many commercial software processes are being realized, and fewer programmers are needed now to implement a big computer system.

It is a general trend in information technologies that you need to know less overall, but that information that you do need to know is much more specific. It's much more condensed, and it's much more functional. It's oriented towards the software that you're using. Basically, you don't need to know machine language programming and C++ to start working in plant maintenance.

With these layers removed, all you need to know is what's in this book. This is the part of the software you need to know. Take, for instance, SAP plant maintenance. I want you to understand how exciting these interview books are as a resource to help you do your job in SAP. For plant maintenance, you flip through and find the subject headings in the table of contents, which will point you towards those topics. When you start to see topics repeated, you know they are important. For example, just by looking at the table of contents for this book, you can see that PM orders and functional order are important.

Now these interview question books are excellent because they tell you what people are really talking about. After you see the prominence of a topic, after you see questions about assigning stock to a PM order, you know that this is the place to start your investigation into PM.

In preparation for an interview for a job utilizing PM, you need to note everything about PM orders, storage locations, activity for plant cost, PM order creating notifications, equipment master, maintenance orders, the planning plant, post-pulmative order, etc. What you're trying to do is read every question and read every answer and make a mental note of this. As you're reading through these questions, you'll see that some things pop up more than others. These are the things to remember. It is absolutely pivotal to remember the popular topics and issues during an interview.

The index is an alphabetical list of the important topics in the book, such as: access control, accounting indicator, automatic warranty, billing plan, and some transaction codes are included here.

This is the anatomy of the interview questions book. This book serves as a heuristic to help you identify what's important for you to study, what's important for you to know, and what you don't need to know.

If you compare that to an SAP Press book, which is the big fat textbook that has everything, you will easily see the difference. I recommended you buy those and read everything, but it's hard to know what's important and what's not, and that's what you get from these interview books. They help you understand what you need to know and what you can safely ignore. These books are small and may be criticized by some for not having that much information, but that's not what these books are all about. These books are about providing answers to specific topics, not providing answers to every possible question. If you want all the information, it's freely available on http://help.sap.com.

Interview books are time-saving resources. You can, for example, just flip through and can instantly tell what the most important things are in PM. Then, go into an IDEZ system for PM and learn everything about creating a PM order from scratch. This is the best way to prepare for an interview.

I wouldn't suggest using these books on the actual interview call. For example, if they ask you a question about transaction code OIOA, you wouldn't want to say, "Hold on a second. Let me go look that up." That just won't work.

So, that's just a little bit about the interview questions book. They're so powerful because they provide important content in a very small package.

You don't have to read the 500-page SAP Press book, although I do recommend doing so. Afterwards, refer to the interview questions book to see the most important topics for your skill set, and then you'll know where to focus your efforts, and that will enable you to have more successful interviews, which is what this book is all about.

Interviewing

This chapter is about interviews: how I prepare for an interview and how I recommend preparing for an interview.

You need a dedicated space to perform your interviews. I've done interviews in my car. I've done them driving on the freeway. I've done them in cafés. And I've lost my fair share of interviews.

When I was first getting started in my career, I was devastated if I didn't get the job. Why didn't I get it? There are all sorts of reasons, and you can't expect that you're going to win each one. In the SAP business, most of your interviews and hiring decisions will happen over the phone. You may never meet these people face-to-face.

I always felt that I would interview better in person because I feel that I have many strengths that are communicated face-to-face, but this is not how the SAP business works. Everything is done over the phone and there might be ten people in a conference room on the other end of the line. You try to make a personal connection with these people, and it's just impossible, and people are firing questions at you left and right.

The other thing to remember is that there's a whole political situation going on at the potential client, that you have no idea about. Out of these ten people, they may have one expert that says, "We really need an MM purchasing person that also has variant configuration experience." And that one person is sort of a bully, and everybody else really knows that the employee doesn't need variant configuration. That's not an aspect of the business. But this one guy, since he says they need variant configuration, somebody asks you, "Do you know variant configuration?" If you say "I haven't seen this used in a dozen years" you're out of the running.

There's a whole political situation that's going on with your client that you have no idea about. You have no idea what they're looking for. During your interview, it's going to be your job to try to understand more, but you're not going to land every job. So the goal is to do as many interviews as possible. If you want to remain consistently employed in SAP, remember the code ABI: Always Be Interviewing.

You should interview once a week. I understand you're going to have engagements that last six months. However, I can't overstate the importance of the skill of interviewing, so that you remain consistently engaged. In the world of independent contracting, you need to be employed all the time, so you go from contract to contract. It can be very lucrative, but you're going to do a lot of interviewing. The longevity and success of your career depends largely on your interviewing skills.

Some people only want to get a permanent job in SAP working for a very big company, and be there for their entire career. However, I don't think it's a viable career path. I think big corporations don't have any loyalty to their employees. They may give it lip service and say, "Oh, this is a great place to work," but at the end, if there are cuts in IT, you may find yourself without a job just like that, and what do you do if you've committed so many years to one of these companies?

Another way to think about this is that your ability to interview is like job security. It is a great peace of mind to know that you have skills that you can take anywhere and employ yourself with, and this is one of the great reasons to be in SAP and IT. Yes, it's a global market. We live in a global world now and you're competing against people all over the world.

The rich west is competing with emerging economies. While this scares a lot of people, it doesn't scare me. I think there's a great deal of opportunity, and it's exciting because your next job might be in Europe, it might be in America, and it might be in Asia. Change is constant in this world, so I view this constant interviewing as a positive. We have to think of it in terms of, "This is my job security, and this makes me a more marketable person, and if my superior at this company is a gigantic pain, I won't be working here very much longer. I can take these skills on the global market, and I can go work in London, Los Angeles, Paris, and Tokyo. I can go work anywhere."

I hate to be melodramatic about this, but that's really what's at stake with interviews. That's why I've dedicated the last several years of my life to developing the interview. I think by recent accounts, we've published approximately 30 books in SAP and over 100 interview questions books, because I view that as the skill of the future. Not that interviewing alone is the skill, but it's certainly how you communicate your skill. It's certainly how you get hired. So if you're in SAP, if you're in IT, if you're working in IT and plan on making your future in this, you must master interviewing skills.

I want to talk about some of the techniques that I run into called black hat techniques. They're dishonest, unethical and unprofessional. If I'm interviewing somebody that's employing these techniques, I won't work with them. I won't work with their firm ever again. You need to know what to look out for.

The first technique is having a recruitment company sit in on the interview on your behalf. The client hires you, and then you suddenly show up and go do the job. This is deeply unethical.

I think the news is out on this, and people are starting to ask for birth dates, social security numbers, etc. I've sent pictures in before, and have taken my picture when I had an interview so it could be sent to the client. The game is up on this one.

Another technique I've seen is called jamming. In this case, you have somebody on three-way calling and you're on instant messenger. You're asked a question and your buddy hears it, types in the answer, or the hot buttons, the things you need to talk about, and boom, there you've got it. You could also have somebody conference in, be on a speaker phone, or have some other way of sharing your interview. As you're going through the interview, your buddy is up there pointing with a laser pointer, showing you what to say.

Those are just a couple techniques that some people are using. They are all completely unethical. I think that there is a basic assumption that when you're interviewing, it's your skills and preparation being discussed, and that you are not being coached.

Who knows? Maybe this will be open in the future and work will be done more collaboratively, but I do think it's unethical for a recruitment company to interview on behalf of the candidates. I have to say that the bar has been raised for the quality of the interviews because this is what you're up against. There are people doing unethical things in interviews, but it's causing them to be successful in interviews. How do you compete with that?

So do you decide not to compete at all? That's the other option; in which case, start looking for another job. But I don't think that's the answer, and I think you can be competitive. Honesty is always the best policy, and in my interviews, if I don't know something, I tell them I don't know it, and I'll also give an explanation about my opinion of the importance of the question.

For example, somebody will ask me, "Have you installed SRM with [a particular scenario] and with Seuss invoice?" And I'll say, "No, I have not done that, but I've installed SRM and I've installed Seuss, so there's no reason to believe I couldn't install invoicing." If I don't know the answer, I'll say, "I don't know the answer to that, but I could certainly look it up, and as a foremost expert in this area, I don't know anybody that could give you the answer off the top of their head." Now it's not appropriate to say that in all circumstances, but in some cases, it is. I think it's appropriate to guide your interviewers' inappropriate instances and tell them what is appropriate to ask and what's not appropriate to ask. And maybe you'll say, "I don't know," and leave out an explanation. Yet if you do say "I don't know", I recommend giving an explanation.

The more experience I gain in this work, the more I know what is okay to say. Rather than make something up, I'd much rather hear, "I don't know, but I know where to look to get the right answer" or "I don't know, but I'd rather take the proper time to look this up."

When I prepare for an interview, I use a white board and I divide it up into quadrants and I try to develop a story.

Past, present, future, and skills: those are my four quadrants. Past includes things that I've done in the past. For example, MM, writing interfaces, writing ABAP. I'll write down the names of previous clients, and what I did for each client. Present includes what I'm doing right now. Right now, I'm working on the SRM for a client and I'm implementing [these scenarios]. The future includes what I'd like to do and the technology being implemented by my target client. In my interview, I'm connecting past, present and future and I'm telling a story about how I'm combining all these technologies and why I'm the best candidate for the job using my skills from the past, and the skills I use now.

The final quadrant is skills, and these are things that are very technical, such as transaction codes. Not that a transaction code is overly technical, but in an interview, it is. You're going to want to write things down in the skills column that you think they'll ask you. If you take my recommendation and pick up at least one interview question in this book, you'll see jargon. You'll see tables, transaction codes, cost centers, and much more. Write these things down in the Skills quadrant, even if you don't know how important they are. These are buzzwords, to lend credibility to what you're saying.

I think it's worth explaining to people why you're interested in a job. For example "One reason I'm really interested in this job is because I've implemented SRM with Seuss in the past. I did a prototype of the invoicing that your company wants to implement, and I'm very excited to have the opportunity to work on this. You can see in the past I did this, in the present I'm doing this, and in the future, I'll very clearly be able to do this other thing."

So, put your past, present, future and skills on a white board, up in the front so that when you're taking your phone call, everything is clear. I also have a written piece of paper, single–sided, with all the transaction codes, and I have another sheet of paper with the major process flows. Depending on your area, there may be two or three process flows, but I find it very useful to have a printed flow chart of the process to come back to and to reiterate the process flow over and over.

It shows how conversant you are with the module. It's also a good way to prep for very specific questions such as, "What if a cost center doesn't show up on a shopping cart?" If you say, "Let me think about that for a second," they're going to try to stump you. Instead of that, you need a mechanism to talk about. "Well, let me see if I understand what you're talking about. You ask me what about a cost center that doesn't show up in a shopping cart...?"

I'll use SRM as my example. SRM is a self-service procurement with a shopping cart. The user logs in and goes to their shopping cart. They add an item to the shopping cart. Are we talking about a material master item? Are we talking about a free flow text item? Maybe they'll say, "Oh, a text item." Okay, so I've added a text item to the shopping cart. I go to fill out the cost center details. Are you talking about a predetermined account assignment category? Then they'll say, "Okay, well, the account assignment category is WPS."

This way, you'll be able to walk through the process. "So I've logged in. When a user logs in, they have pre-assigned assignment categories that are defaulted for each user, so has that been configured?" From the start, you can ask a dozen questions. You can ask them a dozen more questions about their question, and then they'll give you an answer.

"Yes, the user has been assigned an account in assignment category for WBS." And then, "Okay, great, so we've added an item. I've created my shopping cart and I've added my item. I'm going to the account assignment category, WS. Now WBS, this is a project systems element, and I know by default there is no drop down for WBS. So it's in SAP, and that's not going to be supported. So if you want one, you need to do a custom development to do a search help on W."

What I'm really trying to communicate is that I know the mechanism. You know, I happen to know the SRM process flows in my head forward and backwards, and that's why I can talk about it with you like this, but if this is an area you're just getting started in and you're breaking into SAP, you need that process flow in front of you.

Really good interview questions are challenging. Your interviewers will ask you a question about your skills, and you must be able to talk about them. This is a good mechanism you can use to ace an interview: have a copy of that process flow in front of you.

The other thing that you want to have is a copy of your resume. That sounds really simple, but I've been working in SAP for a dozen years now and my resume is about eight pages long. You may be asked "What in your past experience qualifies you for this job?" You can memorize your resume, or you can simply refer to it and respond, "Oh, okay, I think the work I'll be doing for you is very similar to the work I performed when I worked at General Mills in food production. Food manufacturing doesn't seem very similar to the work you do at the U.S. Army, but they are basically two very large logistical organizations, and at the core, that's your business."

If you have your resume, you can look back. If you forget, that might cause you to hesitate on an answer or become nervous. This can lead the interviewer to say, "When he was talking about his past experiences, he hesitated and he got nervous. Maybe he just made that up."

If you've been working for a while, you can't remember everything you've done in the past. You need to have it written down, and you need to have a copy there for yourself. Many times, your resume is the only thing the client has, so your interviewers are looking your resume and listening to your voice on the phone. It's up to you to bring that to life. I would recommend that at least one time during the interview, you say, "Hey, if you refer to this page on my resume, you can see this sort of experience." Use your time with them as an opportunity to point out something that's beneficial about your resume. On your white board, you'll have a few talking points from the past that will very easily allow you to do this.

I want to close this chapter with something about the kinds of people that are desirable in SAP.

I was talking earlier about an interview where I had 10 people on the phone, and they were in a conference room, and it was just me on the phone versus a team. I gave an answer and I know that at least one person hated it, but they asked me a specific question that was ridiculous. I answered, "I haven't skipped on my left foot down the right-hand side of the street whistling this song backwards, but, I don't think anybody should be required to do that either, so I feel completely confident in my ability to do what you've asked. This scenario is something I've done one way too many times, and there's no reason that I can't do this." I didn't get that job, but I chalk it up to the fact that I wouldn't want to work at a place like that, where they're going to browbeat somebody. You may have these types of interviews, and if you are prepared, you may avoid this situation all together.

When people ask questions with such specificity, I consider them bad employers. They're trying to tell everybody else at the table how smart they are. I think my problem with answering that question is that I was a little bit too honest and too forward. I should have backed off and said something such as, "Oh, wow, that's such a complicated scenario. I'm not sure. I'd have to do some extensive testing about this. Have you actually encountered this? Is this something that you're trying to do?" Then the interviewer will say, "Oh, yes, I'm very smart. I know everything, and I can't believe we're even trying to hire somebody because I know it all." So you have to be aware of people like that, especially in these conference room settings. This is a prime example of internal politics.

So you may end up on a call where you encounter this kind of a person, but try to treat them as gently as possible. Maybe act surprised. "Oh, really, wow, that's such a complicated scenario. It's exciting to me. This is a challenge. I've never heard of this before. Maybe this is something new and interesting."

Ultimately, you should be humble in an interview. You have your white board. You have your resources. Be as exact as possible. But if you're running into questions that are overboard, you can act surprised, or you can say, "Well, how interesting." If you happen to have all the answers and you happen to know it all, this is another thing to be careful of. You want to have answers for every question, but in many cases, it's not always the person that knows everything that you want to work with, rather it's the person that knows where to get the answer to things they don't know.

It's important to be a resourceful person, who, for example, maybe knows the guy at SAP who is working on this. You can say, "If there ever is a problem that I encounter, I have a personal relationship with the developer, and I can call him to get the answer" or "I know somebody in Germany on [XYZ development team] and I can call them personally" or "I've read every book on this topic. I have many friends working in this area. "

I'd rather talk to somebody that's resourceful than somebody who knows it all. I'd rather interview somebody who is honest and down to earth and somebody that I might want to be friends with than somebody who knows it all. This will change from client to client, but you score a lot of points on an interview if you can say things like, "That's a really interesting question, and I'd rather not give a wrong answer. Let's talk about it. Let me talk through this question."

If you get stuck, I think you'd score for saying, "I'd rather not give a wrong answer here. If it's very important, I can find out and get back to you." A lot of times in interviews, they'll ask you questions that they themselves don't know the answer to. If you start to have a dialogue, they'll say, "Well, have you done this? How about this? How does that work?" In this case, if you don't know the answer, giving a wrong answer is far worse.

The last thing I'll say is that you want to work with people who care about the things they're doing. When talking about the future, say, "Yeah, I'm interested in this. I'm excited about this technology. It's something I'm excited about doing, and I'd really like to take this job."

Chapter Three

Negotiation

This chapter is about negotiating the best contract possible and making sure that your work is recognized, because how companies recognize your work is by paying you and by paying you well. One way to ensure that you're paid well is by negotiating your contract.

This sample contract discussion is with a consulting company called Extrinsic. It's their standard consulting contract. I'm not sure how well-known they are, but Extrinsic is a player mostly in the U.S. health sciences field in SAP. After being a team leader for them on a project and successfully installing SRM at a Fortune 500 client, Extrinsic decided that they weren't going to pay my last month's bill, which totaled about $20,000.

This was after I had extensively negotiated this contract and had done a pretty good job at making sure that my contract didn't include any zingers or any big problems. At the time, I was very upset that they weren't paying my bill, but I was thinking to myself, "What if I hadn't negotiated this contract as well as I had?"

I've been bitten before, and this is why I always review every last clause in every contract I sign, because there could be something in there that is absolutely unacceptable. I urge you never to sign a contract that has any unacceptable clause. In the very minimum, what you really want to do is negotiate each term, and if something's unacceptable, send the contract back to them saying, "Please review this. I can't work under this contract."

At the very minimum, cross it out. Then sign it and send it back to them if you don't feel like you're in a place of strength or negotiation, or write a big question mark right on top of the clause in the contract you don't like and put your initials by it.

In the minimum, this technique will protect you later. If you put a question mark on there, it indicates you didn't understand this contract, and that could save you or it could open a later negotiation. You say, "I didn't understand the contract, and if you look at the copy I signed, you'll see that on page number three, there's a question mark. So do you want to go to court over this contract? It says right there I didn't understand what I was signing, but you insisted that I sign." So that's another sort of a tactic you can use to negotiate.

However, you really need to review the whole thing and be sure there aren't any big problems.

SAP INTERVIEW QUESTIONS

I've made the Extrinsic contract available to you, and it's called the Consulting Pack No. 1. You can log in Corp to Corp Agreement in the Breaking into SAP online course.

This is the first copy of this contract, before negotiation. Before continuing, print out a copy of this contract from the consulting pack and come back so that you can look at the contract's language.

Much on the first page is standard. It states this is who they are, this is who you are, it describes the services, and this is what you're going to do as an independent contractor. That's all fine.

Fees and terms of payment is the interesting part.

The only good thing about this contract is if you look at the first part that's highlighted, it says, "Subcontractor will invoice Extrinsic for fees and applicable expenses weekly." This is good because as a contractor, you want to bill every week. It's just the best way to keep track of your expenses and to keep track of your time. Send them an invoice with your time every week.

You'll run into contracts where they'll say that you must invoice monthly. If this contract said monthly, that would be the very, very first thing I negotiate as a contractor. Think about it. If you go to work on January 1st, you'll work until January 30th. You send them a bill on January 30th or 31st. Your terms are most likely going to be net 30. That means that you won't get paid for another month. You work all of February, and you finally get paid on February 28th. In this case, you've worked for two months without getting paid.

I don't know how much money you have in the bank, but I can't afford to work for two months extending my valuable time without compensation. Most likely, you're going to be incurring expenses on behalf of your client, so we're talking about 60 days with no income. And how many contracting firms pay on time? Very few.

I've lost contracts over this before because you know these contracting firms and companies are getting wise. They say, "We can have somebody here for two months risk-free. If we don't like the work they do, we'll just tell them to take a hike, and we tear up their contract or we'll find a clause in their contract that they did not adhere to."

That's two months of your consulting time. First of all, it's your livelihood, but you have to protect yourself from being gamed by these guys. And they will do so. I've been gamed in this exact way by Raytheon, one of the biggest companies in the world. You can say, "If they're that big, they have the money to pay you." You still have to be very careful.

Big companies enter into agreements like this purposefully because they don't believe individuals have the wherewithal to battle them legally. For the most part, they're right. I luckily had an attorney that I used to fight Raytheon. Finally I got paid, but it took months and I wound up with about 50% of the original amount due me, after I paid my lawyer. Any time you spend up front in negotiating and making sure the terms of this contract are not totally one-sided is very much worth your time, and I urge you to do so.

I'm not an attorney. I'm not giving you legal advice here. I'm just helping you understand that you can negotiate a lot of this on your own. I personally don't send each contract I receive to my attorney, because it would probably cost $1,000 for every contract. However, there is a lot you can do by just looking at it and saying what works for you and what doesn't work for you.

Please don't just sign a contract and send it back. I would say there's going to be at least five or six things in every contract you'll need to negotiate. The first one is how often you send them an invoice. Billing weekly is the best way to go.

This next highlighted area says, "Upon receipt of subcontractor's invoice Extrinsic will remit payment for all client accepted services and expenses within 30 business days." That's where it says this is a net 30 days (upon receipt of the invoice) term, which is fine. You need to also make sure that you're sending the invoice in the right way. Sometimes they'll say, "We never received the invoices. You didn't send them to us the way we want." So I always ask a client to confirm receipt of an invoice.

If you go to page 3, I'm going to hit one of the most important items in this contract, particularly termination. In my opinion, this is absolutely egregious. It may even be illegal. I would never sign a contract like this. It says, "If subcontractor fails to provide 14 days written notice for reasons other than acts of God, Extrinsic will bill subcontractor $250 a day for each day defaulted during the 14-day termination period. Contractor will be on vacation during period."

Now, the reason I had a real problem with this is because it says if they fail to provide 14 days' written notice for reasons other than for acts of God. That was a little bit too ambiguous for me. What constitutes an act of God? I need to understand more about what would be covered.

Here is a personal story about this contract. My wife was pregnant at this time. I knew we would be having a baby, so this really worried me because let's say there was a complication and she had to give birth early, and I had to leave the contract to take care of my personal family business. Would they have said, "This is not an act of God? This is a personal reason. You didn't give us proper notice. Therefore, we're billing you $250 a day."

Based on my experience with Extrinsic, that is exactly what they would have done. If I had to leave the project for any reason, they would have billed me.

First of all, they would have held any outstanding invoices due me. And then they would not have paid me for the work I did. And then they'd bill me $250 a day. We're talking potentially thousands of dollars here, which is entirely unacceptable. So I negotiated this clause out of the contract.

It's okay to negotiate the contract. If you're at this step, they want to hire you. You just need to make sure that the details are appropriate.

Weekly billing, net 30 terms, and no punishing termination clauses are the absolute minimum. There are many other things in this contract that are frankly bad, and when you get a bad contract, it's a red flag. If they give you a sucker contract like this, you must take care and negotiate it carefully. As you're going through and working the contract, be very careful to adhere to the terms in this contract because they'll hold your feet to the fire.

Billing you $250 a day if you have to leave a project early is ridiculous. In this world, you may have to leave a project for any reason. It's a problem of the contract and contingent workforce. They want it both ways. They want to be able to fire you at a moment's notice, but they want you at their beck and call.

When I'm negotiating a contract, all I ask for is that the terms go both ways. If you can fire me at any time, then I can walk out at any time. If you can terminate me with two weeks' notice, then I will give you two weeks' notice.

You need to make these contracts as two-sided as possible, and don't give away your rights. Don't give away your time for free. You don't have to, and to be honest, they shouldn't ask you to. And if they do ask you, they're being dishonest and unethical and you should think twice about working for a firm that asks you to sign such a contract.

Negotiation Timeline

In this section, I'll talk about what I call the contract negotiating timeline. It sounds like a buzzword, but it's something that I'm always thinking about when I'm applying for a job, interviewing, and then ultimately landing a job in SAP.

From the time you start interacting with a recruiter up until you're done with the contract, your value changes.

This is an extreme example, but we'll say you're on an implementation. Right before you're about to finish your configuration, and right before the project's about to go live, is when your value is the highest.

It's not ethical to go to your project manager at the last moment and say, "I need more money. Otherwise, I'm going to walk." In theory, however, that would be the time when you would be worth the absolute most to that organization because you know they need your expertise. You've been working there for six months, and you know everything about the system, and at that moment you know your leverage would be the highest. If you had to renegotiate a contract, that would be the time.

Renegotiating your contract is ethical and acceptable if your contract is coming up or has ended at an opportune moment. When you're negotiating a contract you should never say, "I'm very happy here. This is the only contract I want to take."

Instead, you say, "I have three or four other contracts and other offers for higher rates. I cannot stay here unless I have a rate increase." That's the extreme example, right in the middle of the implementation.

The first time you talk to the contracting agent, you'll talk to a recruiter or an agency of some sort and they'll ask for your rate. This is when your value is very low, and they'll want to drive your rate as low as possible. Make no mistakes. Recruiters want to get as much of your money as possible. They rely on you not feeling confident about your skills and the value of your skills in the marketplace.

So you'll say, "I need at least $125 an hour." They're going to say, "Whoa. Boy. That's so much. I doubt you're going to get that." You should say, "I think this is what my value is in the marketplace, and I'm confident that if the client sees good value, then they'll hire me."

Again, they'll try to beat you up and convince you that you're not worth that much. They'll say, "We could never get that much. Only the most experienced people get that much." They'll give you any number of stories.

Another thing they'll do is give you a so-called technical interview. This will be held by the recruiter. It won't be the client at all. It'll just be some guy who works for the recruitment agency or another one of their contractors that they've talked to. Many times, it's not even an employee. They'll ask if you can do a technical screen. Really try to go hard on this guy.

Then this guy will ask you a million impossible questions, and then you'll get a call back from the recruiter. The recruiter will say, "I'm not sure that technical interview went very well. I know you were asking for $125, but if you can take $80, I might be able to do this."

The rate that goes to the recruiter is exactly the same. He's just trying an obvious ploy, telling you your skills are low. That guy just made himself $40 an hour, which is a lot of money. Right?

Yet, there is some truth. It's important to know that your value is so low because they haven't committed you in their process. They haven't passed your name to the client. They haven't invested time in working you in their system or talking to you, etc.

This is the time when you have the least amount of power. When you're talking to them for the first time, be really careful and don't commit to a rate. Don't let them beat you down. That's how you negotiate these first interactions with the recruiter. Say, "I'll be happy with..." and use a range.

As you move on, you start insisting. "I need $150. Otherwise, this isn't going to work." This occurs during the second interview and client interview, up until your start date.

After you've started, your value is very high because you're working there. Chances are they want to keep you. They've gone through all the screening and all these other things which are perceived as being a lot of work. They really want to keep you there so you can make more requests, and they'll give you more concessions.

My basic premise is to do everything you can to have a high value point, while committing as little as possible towards the end of the lower-value spectrum. At the very beginning, they'll send you a contract, and they'll ask you to sign to it. I always delay sending that contract back to them.

"I'm still reading it. I'm still looking through it." If you haven't talked to the client, and the client has not expressed interest in bringing you on board, there is absolutely no reason that you should be submitting a contract to anybody. It's just a tactic that they're going to use to tie you down to the worst terms possible.

The sweet spot where you can negotiate with your contracting agency is after you've done the client interview, but before you've rolled on. That's when you want to really step up and say, "Look, I need $10 more an hour. I need to be paid on net 30. I cannot deal with this termination clause. I need to bill every week."

Toward the very beginning, when you start to talk to recruiters, don't tell them what rate you're willing to work at. Give a range. And don't let them tie you down. This is where your interests and the recruiter's interests are absolutely at odds. On the other hand, you need to convince the recruiter that you're at least a little bit flexible, because if you say, "Nope. I'm at this rate and these are my terms," as the market tightens, they'll start to say, "We can't deal with this person. They're too difficult." They want to work with people they can walk all over. They want to work with people that will accept whatever terms, whatever crappy contract they're trying to push. That's their first choice.

You might pretend a little that you are willing to work with them and be a little bit flexible. And then after you've convinced the client of your value, the negotiation really starts. Do not sign your contract before the client has given them the okay because that's when you have all the leverage.

In some cases, the recruiters or contract agencies will try to get you to sign your contract when your value is low because it's very easy. Don't do it! Put in your question marks before you send it back to them. That's not a fully executed contract and they're going to want to go back. Then, have your client interview. You convince them, and then they're going to want to roll you on. That's when you do your final contract negotiation.

There's a timeline that moves all the way from when you start talking to a recruitment agency until you've rolled onto a project, and afterwards. Your value follows a curve. At the very beginning, it's worth very little. Then it goes up and up until the point where you're going to roll onto the project. That's your peak negotiating time.

Once you get onto the project, it dips down a little bit because you're there. You're engaged with the client, and it's very difficult for you to convincingly say, "I'm going to walk unless you improve these terms." Once you've gone onto the project, you've already agreed to all the terms.

In many ways, going back on your original agreement is not okay. But if you happen to be on a contract by the time your contract terms expire, it is okay to go back and ask for more.

Be aware of this timeline and be aware that it's not to your advantage to sign anything until you have the go-ahead to continue. Right before you start the project is when your value is the highest, and that's when you need to make sure that you have a good rate and payment terms. Make sure everything is good.

The other thing that is unspoken is once you've established a relationship with the client, they're going to want you, and if the deal doesn't happen, they're going to wonder what happened. Maybe the contracting agency is trying to cut you out; if that gets back to the client, they may want to hire you through a preferred vendor or directly.

Let's say the recruiter said, "No, it didn't go well. They don't want you unless you'll work for $80 an hour." Meanwhile, the company is paying the recruiter $150. These games happen all the time. However, those games will be up, and that recruitment agency will be out with the client after that. If it happens to you, try to get a hold of the client and tell them, "They're trying to hold my feet to the fire in this contract. They're not paying me an appropriate rate." For the right people, those contract issues work themselves out.

Be aware of the timeline. Use it to your advantage. And negotiate every contract, and try to get the most because the recruiters are doing the same to you. They're employing every tactic in the book to convince you that you are not worth anything and that your value in the marketplace is very low. So you have to fight back.

The underlying philosophy is you have to know and believe that your time is valuable. If they're not willing to pay for it, there are plenty of other places to go. And this is where the contracting market will be a little bit scary and harder on contractors.

Yet, IT is in demand, and there are plenty of jobs out there. I've never had to give in on my contract terms, even during the hardest markets, and neither do you. IT skills are very much in demand and you can command the highest rates, but it's up to you to negotiate those terms.

Recruiters are going to tell you, "Oh, the market's different." I've been hearing this for ten years. It's different. It's changing. Demand's low. There are a lot of people in the market. It's flooded. Basically, are they going to convince you that you're not worth anything?

You just say, "I know what my needs are, and this is what it's going to take for me to take the job. And if I don't have it there, I've got plenty of offers." This goes back to something I said earlier: always be interviewing.

If you want to remain consistently employed and have the strongest position from a negotiation standpoint, you should have your resume out there at five or six different legitimate projects that you could possibly go to at any given time.

For me, I get three or four calls a day, minimum, from recruiters. And I've even taken my consulting profile down and have gone low profile.

So if you're actively soliciting business and trying to get SAP contracts, your phone will probably be ringing off the hook.

The most important message is: at the very beginning, they're going to hammer you. So don't commit to a rate.

Don't commit to terms. Just wait until you talk to the client. After you talk to the client, then start negotiating the contract so that you have the best terms possible.

In some cases, you may be able to do that even after you start, although you have to be very careful not to be perceived as going back on your original agreement. If you sign a contract, you need to honor that and work the duration at the rate that you agreed upon.

Now if something in the contract changes, it expires, it ends during the term, then they can come back and renegotiate. But you say, "I've got three or four other places to go. I can get a better rate. So if you can step up, then I can say otherwise." It's a little bit of a poker game. You have to be willing to walk. And ultimately, that's your power here. You can never negotiate unless you're willing to walk away from the table.

Your only chip in the game is your time and the skills that you bring to the table. And if you're not willing to stand up and walk away, then you have very little power, and you're not going to negotiate good contracts. Your ability to step up away from the table depends on how hot your skills are, how good you are at marketing yourself, and getting your resume out there.

If you legitimately have three or four offers, it may seem like you're playing poker, but you're not because you have three or four other people to talk to. You can bounce your rate off these other people and get the rate that you want.

So don't limit yourself and just start working with one. If there's only one job, keep trying to get other jobs. Because if you have three or four things lined up, then one will definitely come out of that. I think of it like a funnel. I'm filling the funnel with as many opportunities as I can. One will eventually come through.

If you have three or four going on, you can stick to your rate and not commit to a lousy contract right out of the gate. Employ these tactics so that at the last minute you can extract the best terms and the best rate and make all this worth your while. Because it can be very much worth your while.

On a contract, you should be making two to three times what you'd be making as a permanent employee, and I think that's worthwhile.

Contracting

As we start to talk about contracting, one of the first things you'll notice is not everybody's making the same rate on the project. You may be making $70 an hour, but the guy next to you might be making $150 an hour.

Not only is that not fair, it's impossibly aggravating. You might even be working harder than this other guy, and you're making half of what he's making. And what you earn doesn't always correlate to the skills that you have or how good an SAP person you are. It's all about how you negotiated your contract.

One of the most important things is to understand the employment landscape. There's the client.

This is the person that you work for. If you work directly for the client, you have a direct client relationship. You'll see ads on Dice that say, "We have a direct client relationship."

Even if these guys are down at the bottom, yes, they have a direct client relationship with the people right above them. In fact, I feel that they shouldn't have to say they have a direct relationship with the client. I tend to think that they're being less than fully honest.

Now it goes without being said that the higher up you are on this chain, the better. Let me walk through a typical scenario. Let's say the client is Ford Motor Company, and their consulting partner is Deloitte & Touche. Deloitte & Touche is running the show. There's a contracting agency called Sojetti that hires all the contractors for Deloitte. There are already two middlemen in front of you getting paid, and taking away from your hourly rate.

If the rate to the client is $150 from the consulting partner, they're going to give the contracting agency $125, and they're going to give you $100. It's pretty clear. The closer you are to the client, the more money is available for your hourly rate.

This is the holy grail of consulting. You have to form relationships with as many people as you can that will help you land clients at the highest level. Unfortunately, it's one of the characteristics of information technology that projects tend to take a long time to be funded. So we're talking about lead time.

Sales cycles are very, very long. You could be waiting on a client for a year and then maybe the project never materializes. So, you can't afford to not be working during this time. How do you battle that?

Well, you can use recruitment agencies to keep you employed. That's their job, in addition to understanding what openings are available, what projects are going on, who's hiring, etc.

However, you have to use recruiters the right way. You can't just trust them to do things that are in your best interest, because they will work to do things in their best interest, and they will always try to get as much money out of you as possible. They're going to try to hold on to your money for as long as possible. And when you roll off the project, they're going to try to not pay you what you're owed.

You need to be very, very careful when approaching a contracting relationship. You need to know where the agency fits on this landscape. Is your recruiting agency working directly for the client? Then it might be something you can be looking into.

Are they tier four? Are they all the way at the bottom? The first thing you need to do as a contractor, if you want to be a success in this business, is quickly learn how to get a feel for what these people sound like and what they say.

People down at this lower end of the spectrum will ask you to sign a non-disclosure or non-compete agreement. They're going to say, "Work only with me. Don't submit your resume through anybody else." They'll tell you things that are just patently untrue. They're false. They don't have anything to do with the price of tea in China, and everything that they tell you is designed to take your money. They're actually doing you direct harm.

Don't listen to what these recruiters say. Everything they say and do is designed to keep you captive to their firm so that they can take as much money out of you as possible.

This may sound adversarial or that I'm anti-recruiter. I'm not anti-recruiter. However, I'm here for you, and I'm here to help you advocate your own interests. I'm here to help you break into SAP, and part of that is learning to manage as a contractor, learning how to manage your employment engagements. Increasingly, there will be contracts, which are something you must learn to manage yourself.

When I was just getting my start, it happened to me many times. I've spoken with "Breaking Into SAP" students. If you're working with a third or fourth tier provider, you're just not going to get paid. You have a check written from here to here. From here to here. From here to here. From here to here. Then to you. If your terms are net 30, meaning that you should be getting paid within 30 days, good luck.

Now also consider that many times you'll be traveling. You'll have to pay for rental car and hotel room out of your own pocket. How are you going to get paid on time to take care of your needs, much less your credit card bills for everything else? With airfares what they are, I can see outlaying if you're on net 30 billables. You work one month. That's 30 days you have to cover everything. Then you'll turn in a bill on the last day of the month. Then you have to wait another month to get paid. You're talking about outlaying in full your expenses for 60 days before you're going to get paid.

You can't go much longer than that. Or maybe you can, but I certainly can't. And you're never wrong in asking these recruiters, "Where do you stand in this whole scheme of things? With whom do you have a relationship?" This is the way you approach it.

I say, "I understand if you can't tell me who your client is. That's not what I'm asking. I'm asking are you sending them a bill? Are you going to be able to pay me on time? If not, this won't work. This just isn't a match." And that's OK.

As an experienced contractor in SAP, you'll have to get used to saying, "I'm not interested. I'm not interested in working with a firm that's a third or fourth tier provider. I'm not interested in working with a firm that can't pay me on time. I'm not interested working with a firm that I can't negotiate a proper contract with, because in this business, the devil is in the details."

And the farther we get along in this, we'll start talking about contracts and terms and the common terms that you'll see. The ones that are poison pills. The dangerous things that you just cannot sign.

What I'm really thinking about here are these early termination clauses. Some of these clauses state that if you terminate within 90 days, then you forfeit all outstanding consulting revenues. Are you kidding me? Nobody has three months to give notice in this business. I'd say two weeks, at best. Yet, what if you have a family emergency? You have to travel back home and you can't stay on the project. So you must forfeit your earnings? That's not acceptable to me.

You're going to be trying to work for the client, and again, I think it's the Holy Grail. Maybe it's going to take a lot of luck and a lot of hard work to have all your clients right here, but I think working for these guys is very good. They're reliable.

I mentioned Sojetti earlier, who is wholly owned by Cap Gemini. They place their contracting firm in a foreign country so they can't be sued in the United States, so it's an end run. At this point, I should say that all these contracts and machinations are an end run around employing people in the United States. I'm not saying it's good or bad. I'm going to help you use this to your advantage.

Many people would say, "This is all bad. People's benefits aren't being taken care of. Corporations are bankrupting our futures. They're not taking care of our pensions. They're really raking us workers over the coals." That's one opinion.

I'm more of a realist. This is how it is. Barring significant economic or political changes, this is how it's going to continue. This new knowledge makes a certain sense.

I need somebody that can do something very specific for a specific amount of time. That's fine. But you know what? If companies are going to be that specific, and the requirements are going to be so hard, they need to pay for that so that we can manage our lifestyles.

This is why I advise my students: don't cut your rates and always emphasize quality. Something I've said over and over is, "Yes, I am not the cheapest resource. But you get what you pay for. And if you want somebody of a reasonable quality, you have to pay more for that."

And I'm not competing against people at lower rates. I will not compete. I keep my rate very high, and you know what? I always get my rate. They might shave a couple dollars off, and there's always room to work on it, but I will not work for significantly less than what I need to make a living in this business. So what else is there to say?

You'll hear of not getting paid, having to leave contracts, having to leave early.

They'll use tactics like saying, "Come back for free for a month, and then we'll pay your whole bill." You have to walk away from situations like that. Let me tell you, I've been to Hell and back in this business. Hopefully, you'll benefit from my experiences and not have to repeat my missteps.

SAP Career Paths

I want to talk about career paths, and I'll start by telling you a bit about my career path. We've talked about permanent employees, contractors, and consultants. Now I'll talk more about the specifics of what happens in SAP.

When I got started in the mid-90s, I was a UNIX systems programmer, and I was able to apply working for a company working in SAP. I didn't even know what SAP was. I showed up to do UNIX work and they said, "We have this SAP thing. You're going to have to learn it." So they sent me to training, and I understood very quickly that there was a great deal of opportunity in learning applications.

The more technical you are, the more buried you are in an organization. I understood right away that you want to be working as close to the way a business makes money as possible. My first job was as a UNIX systems programmer at Yamaha Motor Corporation.

This has nothing to do with Yamaha's business. Yamaha makes most of their money, as it turns out, selling parts. Of course, you need information technology to keep track of parts. Translating that to SAP means used store parts and MM, a material master. So I knew that this was an important thing to learn.

Yet, I was a UNIX guy. I wasn't even working in SAP. I very quickly decided that it was my goal to learn SAP and to transition to working in SAP as soon as possible. So I went from UNIX to being an SAP programmer. I was writing programs in ABAP and then I knew: well, okay, Yamaha isn't in the ABAP business. They're in the parts business.

So I instantly saw that my progression, if I were to continue working at Yamaha, would be to move out of the technical areas into working directly with motorcycle parts. Or something working on the most important function in the IT area for parts.

Clearly, it was not writing shell scripts or backing up the UNIX OS or the Oracle database, etc. I understood that I needed to become as functional as possible, as quickly as possible.

I think that's a pretty good model for an SAP career. Start technical and move functional. Now that might not work for everybody. Not everybody has the desire to become a functional consultant. There are plenty of good technical jobs in SAP, but I'm here to talk about how you can break into SAP. Career paths play a big role in this because you can take advantage of market imperfections to break in and land a job, and then to move up quickly and secure yourself a safe position.

The way you need to break into SAP is start technical, and then go functional. For example, master data management (MDM) is a fairly new area in SAP and it's relatively hot. You'll see requirements for MDM catalog people, MDM Java, so these are relatively technical topics. And if you can learn enough of the technical jargon and enough of the technical underpinnings of the MDM product, you could get a job in MDM relatively easily and very quickly because very few people know this.

Now you're probably going to be working in a technical capacity...and that's fine. But as soon as you're on that job, you're thinking, "How can I transition to get some functional knowledge?" And MDM plays well with, for example, MM and SRM. MDM can touch anywhere you're touching master data.

You can then select one of these other functional areas. This might be a little bit of a divergence, but I tend to want to be working on a system that is doing transaction processing. An MDM project has to do with harmonizing data, deleting old records, bad data, etc. Yet at its core, MDM is not in the path of a core business process, like the earlier example with motorcycle parts. MDM isn't going to be motorcycle parts for Yamaha.

MDM is going to be cleaning house on IT and sweeping the floors of an IT shop. SRM, on the other hand, is going to be the procurement of parts that Yamaha is going to sell. That's a part of their business, and it's the same with MM.

Remember the strategy: start technical and go functional. If you're breaking in, you have no experience. So, find a small area, such as MDM, and get the job. Learn as much as you can about SRM, and your next job will be working in SRM functional; and you'll have that MDM experience to put on your resume.

There are much more traditional career paths in SAP, as well. In broad strokes, you start as a programmer, then a technical lead, then an architect. In the functional, you'll be a functional consultant, then a team lead, and then a project manager. Those are two very common career paths.

I'm not mentioning permanent versus contractor versus consultant because that's the nature of the employment itself. You can be a team lead, and you can actually be working as an employee, a consultant, or a contractor. The type of worker you are is just the mechanism of how you're employed. However, the career path is something a bit different.

Let me leave you with those two thoughts. The first step is to start technical and then move to functional. The second step is to work on a business process important to the core of a company. These two things will help you get your foot in the door, and they're also very important in the longevity and the success of your SAP career.

Training

Everybody is afforded the same clean slate, and how we deal with it is up to us. If you're able to really get to know somebody or talk to them honestly about how they got their start in IT, it always is, "I saw a job for this skill. It paid a ton of money, and so I went and bought every book on the topic, practiced on my own. I got the job, and then I learned it all on the job."

I'm a manager and I've had as many as 60 employees, and I was in network operations. I went from networks into SAP, by way of word of mouth. There was a position with *The New York Times,* and they asked if I would be interested, and I said yes.

It was a hard decision because it was my first consulting job.

I've never been without benefits. I'm used to being a permanent employee and having all things that afforded to me. Contracting was a big, eye-opening move for me, but I accepted it so I could see what it was like, because I'd always wanted to. And my children are grown and in college, so I said I could go ahead and give it a try. My husband had benefits, so I didn't have to worry about that. So we talked about it and I decided to give it a try.

I love where I'm at now and I'll be sorry to leave when my contract ends this month, and the client pays me directly. When I was in New York, my money was being transferred three times over. It was ugly. I then had to actually sue someone to recoup my expenses.

In my dozen years, I've been contracting my whole time. That's becoming more and more common.

It was awful. I rolled off early because I wasn't getting paid on time, and after I rolled off, I never got my money. I'm currently in litigation. And it's a cut and dry case.

This is something that people need to know about. There are a lot of mom and pop consulting firms around. One lady called me last week, and I heard dogs barking in the background, babies crying, and I thought, "Who are these people?"

It makes me so mad because I don't know who the end client is. They won't reveal it. A lot of times, they won't tell me so I'm sitting there thinking, "should I do it? Should I trust these people? Because I can't trust anybody anymore."

If you have three layers, good luck getting paid. So I try to avoid that at any cost. I advise people not to do it. Right now I send my invoice to the company, and they pay me directly, net 45 days. I just don't know if I'm going to get paid. One guy brought up that during the contract negotiations, you can add that if they pay you within 30 days, you give them a 2% discount. If they pay you over 30 days, on or after the 31st day, you charge them an extra 1–2%. So you can try to get that added in. It gives them an advantage to want to go ahead and pay you early so they'll get that discount. There is a contracting firm that has a graduated schedule. For example, if we pay you net 15, then we take 5%. If we pay you net 30, we take 3%.

And you'll have these clauses that if you don't provide 90 days notice if you leave the project, then all of your consulting revenue for those 90 days accrues.

Do you understand? It accrues to the contracting firm. These types of contracts are just utterly ridiculous.

For my current litigation, I'm charging court costs and fees. I was going to try to add interest, but I don't know if the judge will let me since it wasn't in the contract.

You can only go after the layer right above you. That's crazy because he's gotten paid by the other guy. There's *The New York Times*, then DG Systems, GTT, then Power Connects, and then me. There are four layers. Also, it's a client that I would return back to. I have been in touch with them, and they say, "We can't do anything." They were actually talking about me coming back – *The New York Times.*

And they don't want to pay me directly. They want me to go through someone else because they don't want the hassles with payroll and with the accounts payable and all that, so they actually have to use a firm. It's like, "We have sub-contractors that have to pay our people and they don't, but great. Our hands are clean." That's exactly what they want, so when they told me that, I'm thinking I'm afraid. I'm afraid to do it. I don't know who's good. I don't know who I can trust.

I just want to work with one guy. Back in the day, they had headhunters. One guy, and he was going after you, going after jobs just for you. He worked for you and you paid him. If a recruiter actually told me that these days, it looks bad. They have to market you. I think that's ridiculous. You can market yourself any way possible. Recruiters are like the middlemen and they want you to do a whole host of things that commit you to them. For instance, they'll ask you to sign a non-disclosure and non-compete agreement that binds you. They'll say, "I'll work for you. I won't talk about this." When you get submitted to a company, they'll say you won't tell them who you're working through.

There was this guy who was also working on the project, so he was getting all the money from all the trainers, plus he was working there too. He was making $300, maybe $400 an hour – serious money. And *The New York Times* didn't know it. The project manager was actually the owner of the company that is providing the service. It's a conflict of interest and probably illegal.

That was my first experience with SAP, and it wasn't pretty. The interesting thing is that all these machinations that we're all talking about, that's how contracting is done, how those services are bought and sold, and how recourses are brought on. Increasingly, if you don't know how to navigate that whole situation, you'll end up three layers down, and it's not workable because you won't get paid.

Everybody, even the newbies, needs to know that. They don't know, and they're willing to do anything to just break into SAP.

So I had to sacrifice myself, but I knew the main thing I got out of it is an education. I learned not only what to do, but what not to do. I guess you go through that once—just once—and hopefully the tuition is low. I've had the same thing happen to me, and it cost me tens of thousands of dollars.

You have high expenses especially when you're traveling: air, hotel. And when the job is done: pay me. I'm up there working, humping for you, and I expect to get paid.

I always make sure the first thing I ask is: "Who are you working for? Are you working for the client? Are you working for another consulting company? Another contractor? How many layers am I going through here?"

And they'll say it's a direct client. Yet this is a buzzword that you'll hear. And then I say, "You're not telling me who your direct client is." Everybody has a direct client. Tell me who you're working for. And if it's not the end user, or if they hem and haw, or if they don't give you an answer, don't work with that firm.

That's what made me write you that night that I sent you that email. I got frustrated. I talked to somebody with a job. It was Lockheed. And this guy—the name of his firm is IH Consultants. I'm like, "Who are you?" And then I asked him who processes the payroll. He says, "Oh, I do." My reaction was: "Oh, that's scary." There's no way.

So it's like you have Lockheed as the client. Deloitte and Touche is the consulting partner. And then you have another guy. In that case, I'd work for Deloitte and Touche. They can pay me as a contractor.

Each of these big major consulting firms like Deloitte and Touche, Accenture, etc.—they all have one designated, big subsidiary. But it's a big company. It's not some dude processing payroll out of his house. So it's probably going to go up through another layer, then. So in this case, you have the client. Then you have the consulting partner. Then you have Segetti. That's okay, because these subcontracting firms, like I said, are wholly owned subsidiaries of the big implementation partner. And you can trust that you will be paid, no problem. But if you go a layer below that, then forget it.

If you have your client, then Deloitte, or if you have your client, then Cap Gemini, and then Segetti, that looks like it's three layers, but that's actually a workable situation because Deloitte and Segetti are the same thing. The client pays them, and then they pay you. That's okay. And you want to work for the big consulting partners. Yet, a lot of times, you'll have Ford Motors, Cap Gemini, Segetti, and then the guy in his backyard, and you're like, "Forget it."

So my philosophy is if you're not going to tell me who the client is, I'm going to hang up the phone. Because I understand that the client is an asset you want to protect. Because if I find that out, I'll call the hiring manager and say, "Hey, I've got these skills. I'll be down there today." I realize that's confidential. But how many layers are there between them and the client? I need to know. And if you don't tell me, I'll never work for you.

The other thing is, they're going to ask you to have an exclusive such as, "I'm submitting you to this client. Don't have anybody else submit you."

It doesn't mean a damn thing, pardon my speaking so directly. Because of course the recruiters want you to work with them and them only. But you know what? You can submit your resume through ten different recruiters all to the same client. The client can choose who they want to work with.

Let's say you're the client. And you're sitting at your desk and you're looking at these resumes from different companies, and you see Martina Ford, Martina Ford, Martina Ford, and Martina Ford.

This kind of thing doesn't look bad at all. In fact, I've been on the other side as a hiring manager and owning a contracting company, and to me, it just means well, okay. And if that resume happens to be a good one and it's qualified, it looks just fine. It looks great and I'll say: "Okay. I guess this is the one."

The management team is going to decide. It's up to them, and in my experience, they choose the contracting firm that they don't have any problems with getting people paid. Because if the customer is the employee or the contractor's not happy, they will not use that guy any more. So recruiters, on the other hand, are going to tell you six ways till Sunday that that looks bad. Because they're losing control. They lose. This whole market is created by an asymmetry of information. Recruiters have the relationship with resources like us. Companies, they don't know anything. They don't have those relationships. Meanwhile, people like us don't know the companies that are hiring. So the recruiters are in the middle, and they're taking advantage of that situation, giving bogus information to people like us and giving bogus information to the companies.

And they do not want us to connect directly, so if you send your resume in four or five times through all these different channels, the client is likely just going to send you an email saying, "Look, we don't know who to use," and they may ask you which recruiter you'd prefer to go through. They may choose the person they like best. In no way does that look bad. It just looks like you're out there and that you're a player in the marketplace.

To recruiters, I was just a number. I felt like a thing, a product, and I didn't feel good. I ripped my profile off Dice as quickly as I could. I just said, "No way, nope, nope, nope. This is not for me. I'll just go the old-fashioned way. Feet on the pavement." Network.

My central philosophy is you don't need so many relationships in SAP. You just need the right relationships. If you have one or two people that can consistently give you jobs or contracts, then you're going to be fine. That being said, finding them is the tricky part.

I'm with CIBA Vision right now which is a pharmaceutical, and they have an account with Dice. They went on Dice, and called me direct. "We want you to come in for an interview, and we'll fly you here." They set it up and it was sweet. Yet now I'm realizing everybody doesn't work that way. So now I want the same deal from someone else, some other company. That's what makes Dice so useful—everybody's on it. You'll get many responses.

Meanwhile, there's a lot of noise. There are a lot of these fourth, fifth tier individuals that are trying to talk you into just working with them, and they'll line you up on a project that you could have found directly yourself. Now if they get a finder fee, that's fine. But just cutting off my pay every day, every month, every hour, I don't like that. But the finder's fee frankly comes out of your pay, too.

This is somewhat on a personal level, but the reason I got out of the contracting business was because it didn't feel right to be benefiting so directly while somebody was being hurt so directly. If I negotiated a rate of $75 an hour, I could charge $150 for them, and every dollar out of their pocket was going into mine, and that was such a direct personal negative adversarial relationship that it didn't work for me.

For instance, I got $50 an hour and then I found out that they were paying $110 for me. And it was just being cut up so many different ways and down to $50. Then I also realized there are other people there that are not going through the same company, and they're making a lot more than me. How does this happen? We're doing the same thing. And *The New York Times* says, "We're paying the same rate for everybody. So however you negotiated your contract is what you got."

I didn't realize how much work was involved and I felt cheated. And that's what made me start investigating so I could know what's going on. Why is my pay so low? I'm doing the same work and even more. I didn't know the game. Now, I do.

These guys are anxious to break into SAP, and they're willing to do anything. They need to know about things like this or they will be taken advantage of.

Someway, somehow, somebody's going to do something. And you won't find out until you're well into it. Then you just have to chalk it up as a learning experience.

Yet it sure is painful and frustrating in the intervening years, and the interesting thing to me is that there are at least a couple hundred thousand people working in this business in the US, and they all must be experiencing the same thing.

The module that I worked with at *The New York Times* was IS Media, which is pretty new over here in the states. So I thought, "This is exciting, this is good. I'm going to some of the pioneers." I think *The Washington Post* and *The Boston Globe* are affiliated with *The New York Times,* so they're also using it. There are only three or four companies that have it implemented. So with that being said, that's what excited me. That's the module that I wanted to master because it was so new and hot over here. And I hear that other companies like Cox have it. It's IS Media. Media broadcast industry. Any kind of a media.

That's where I wanted to stay until I had to roll myself off of that job. If it wasn't because of that, I would still be there. They went live on part of it, and now they're about to go live on the classified section. So they're doing theirs in little pieces. But I wanted to be there, and I feel bad that I didn't stay. Yet, I wasn't getting paid and I couldn't afford the hotel and the flights.

If you're not being paid, there is full and utter justification to walk out. On the very first day I don't receive a paycheck, I go straight to the project manager and say, "I have extended very generous terms to the contracting agency. I haven't been getting paid. I'm running out on my expenses. My credit cards are maxed." You are never wrong for doing that. You can't work for free.

People need to know that they *do* have the power to walk off, even though you feel obligated because you started the job and you want to finish it. That's how I work; I want to finish projects I begin. Yet they're taking advantage of you. I always want to do the best work for my client, and I always advocate my client's best interests, but when they're not advocating my interests, I'm out. If I went to a project manager and said I'm not getting paid, I would expect their jaw to drop, fire the layers, and hire me direct. And if that doesn't happen, then the client's taking advantage of you. We would realize that you're paying your contracting agencies the same rate or whatever, but if they can't make that right, they themselves are taking advantage of you, and you can't continue to go there. You just can't.

But when you go to the client and they say, "There's really nothing we can do, I don't have a contract with them." I have a contract with the agency, so I can walk out. But I don't want to. It puts us in a real bind. What I would say is, "Yes, there is something you can do. You can contract with me directly. You can stop all payments to this contracting firm that's stealing my money."

And that's why I wanted to sue the guy that was right above the guy that was paying me. I asked him not to pay the other guy anymore, to instead just pay me. Give him his cut and give me my cut, but he wouldn't do it.

It puts us in an awfully awkward situation because the only way to resolve this is litigation, and we don't have contracts with any of the people above us in that whole chain. Let me tell you that how I've gotten paid in the past is by suing the client themselves. And more than that, if there's a manager that's making this bad situation happen. You can do this in a small claims capacity, too. Even if they owe you something like $16,000.00. Either sue or threaten to sue the client.

However, I don't want to because they're actually trying to bring me back up there.

So you have the client. Everybody below that is not doing their job. What would happen is you either sue or threaten to sue the client and say, "I don't know what to do. I went to work for you and you're my client. I'm working but not getting paid, so I have no other choice but to sue you."

Then you will find that situation fixed very quickly because if all those other people are not doing their job to the point where the client's going to get sued, then they're going to fix it. Though you can expect that bridge will be burnt.

It is a dilemma, but the thing is it's an individual at *The New York Times*. What you would do is find one person.

If you really wanted to get paid quickly and you didn't want to go through all this, I would say you're going to have to find one person responsible for that whole area. Go down to your local county court, file a small claim against them and then subpoena that person. And when they get served, that will fix that whole deal. Maybe try to convince somebody else to do it that doesn't want to go back to work there.

I keep thinking about the knowledge I gained while I was there, and how I'm applying it now. I'm doing a lot better now.

So now I feel great, even though I'm out some money.

That's the next thing: a project ends. You don't get paid. There's so much energy that goes into collecting payment. And it's intense, negative, disastrous energy.

I don't think there is any excuse for you not getting paid. Straight up. Everybody, including that client, is responsible, and you should feel no guilt whatsoever. They're wrong and you're right. Period.

All that being said, what you've said in your emails to me is that you had acquired several different skill sets. You'd been working in training in several different areas.

I guess the main one was sales and distribution—SD. All aspects of SD as far as accounts payable, credit and collections, credit cards, all that. I wish I could specialize in SD, but it doesn't look like it's really hot. So I want to try to get into something else. That's when I started looking at CRM because I was the manager many years in customer service and network operations. And I still have those qualities such as being customer driven. I was thinking maybe I'll stay with that. I don't know how hot it is right now, but I still see jobs for it.

If SD is not the biggest area in SAP in terms of contracts and permanent employment opportunities, it's the second biggest. I think that's a huge advantage to sticking with SD. If you check Dice, there are 1,000 jobs for SD, and if you rank SD according to all other SAP skill sets, it's No. 1. In terms of the sheer number of jobs, FICO is No. 1. Then BW, HR, and finally SD.

What is the big deal about BW? I just finished a class on Friday, and that was just running queries, but next week, I'll learn how to actually create the queries. It doesn't seem hard to me.

It's not hard at all. It's a very big area because people use analytics and reporting to get the data out of SAP, so everybody needs it. I would not advise anybody to try to get jobs in BW. It's one of these areas that is so technical and you can get into easily and quickly, but it's not connected to any functional area of a business, and it's an area that's been flooded.

There's really not a lot to it, and I have done BW from soup to nuts. I've installed it, created customer info cubes. I feel that I can handle the BW piece of the implementation. People I meet on these projects have zero experience. These guys are gaming the system like you wouldn't believe. Yet the real thing that makes BW a terrible area for people like you is that since you have so much experience in a real functional area, why move to something like BW that doesn't require real knowledge?

People do it because it's easy and it's technical. If I was to ask you, referring to sales and distribution, could you answer the question: "Can you explain to me what the order to cash business process is?"

BW does not have that. BW has a query. It has the different fields and you can tailor it to the client's needs. And there are so many different standard reports already that you can manipulate. It's easy. And these people have trouble even getting that to work. So I look at this list of rankings, and I see that BW is really an outlier because you're not getting paid very much. The jobs are pretty short. It's very, very competitive, and just saturated.

The work is coming from offshore, if you look at it, it's really HR, SD, CRM, and then MM. So I would emphasize

SD as much as possible on your resume. I would say, "I've been working in SD for [however long you feel comfortable saying]." Then I would say, "Most recently, I've been interested in CRM." Because CRM is like SD gold – it's SD, but you get the Web components. You'd be in a really good position to add. And that would be a really logical progression because you had SD, and then you add the CRM piece, and that just makes a lot of sense. CRM's not like BW. It's much harder to learn because you already have to be conversant with the SD process flows to do a good job in CRM. These are the areas with the most overall demand for jobs.

The other concern I had is you say that you've been working in training and you want to transition to a development role or a consultant role. Let's say the score order entry in CRM, and the screens that you see in the GUI in the client. I teach that to the end users of companies implementing SAP. I want to configure that.

I'm a CRM functional consultant. I have a background in SD, and I've been working on projects for six or seven years, which is right in the zone. I have experience designing, implementing and training on these projects. I've been spending six months at each of these projects, and I feel good about that. That's going to be marketable because a lot of people don't have that.

The crazy thing is that people with 5–6 years experience are saying that they have 12 years. They take what they really have and double it. I have 24 years working. I started working SAP when I was 12. So for me, I've still been taking the high road on reporting the number of years. I'll say I've been doing it for 12 years, but if you have 5–6 years experience, that should be enough for any job.

You really harp on specializing. And that's what got me frustrated: I'm not specializing because I'm forced to be all over the place.

I would recommend you have one resume that's going to be your SD CRM resume, and that's all you have on there. Even though I touched all those modules, I can actually separate them in different resumes. When they see the resume, it has to be, "We're looking for somebody with five years of experience in SD." They look at it and there's something else, then they say, "Whoa."

Some companies are implementing different modules, and they may do them at the same time, or they may do them back-to-back. So they know that I can hop from one to the other. When I'm talking with someone, I can just let them know as a side note that I do have other experience, too.

I have my own company. I own a training and development company, and my goal is to have 6–7 trainers work under me, because companies call me to coordinate training and change management. They're looking for someone to come in and lead the trainers and actually help develop the whole training program from start to finish. That's what I do.

Chapter Four

A Day in the Life of an SAP Consultant

This is a light view of a day in the life of an SAP consultant. It's not a bad life, either. During an average week, I would fly out of Los Angeles on Sunday. If my project was in the same state, I'd fly out sometime in the early afternoon, maybe 2:00 or 3:00, show up at my hotel, hopefully within walking distance of my client. Then I'd try to get a good night's sleep.

Traveling through different time zones can be hard on people. I've never had any problem sleeping, however. So, you get up, and you'll be expected to be at work. They're not going to tell you what time you have to be there, although they might say, generally, we get started about such and such a time, probably 8:00. So, that's when you'll be expected to be there.

If you come in at 8:30, people might say, "Oh, boy, this guy's coming late all the time." So, if you come in there at 7:30, that's probably better, but 8:00 is the norm in the United States. I think outside the US might be similar. I was in Australia, and maybe it was a little earlier. I think the project manager had a 6:00 meeting. So, you show up, my day starts, I go get my first cup of coffee.

So, I'm going to get a cup of coffee, bring it back to my desk, and check my email for about an hour or so, looking for meetings, looking for gossip, politics in the office, seeing what's going on with people there. Then after about an hour of checking email, it's about 9:00, and maybe there's going to be a meeting. Functional consultants also have it pretty easy. It's more thought work, and developers are going to be serious coding; but maybe you'll have a mid-morning meeting.

The time between your first cup of coffee and email is maybe spent preparing for a morning meeting, and if you're breaking into SAP, this is your chance to get your books out, find the resources, do the printouts, and study the things you anticipate talking about at the meeting. And in a big project, your area will be quite small. You'll have maybe one thing that you need to address.

So, study up for your morning meeting. Study hard, get everything that you need to know ready, go to the meeting, and try to stay out of the controversy. Don't speak up unless you really know what you're talking about. Or, in the case that you have to lead the meeting, don't let anybody ask you any hard questions. Or just say, "That's too complicated" or "That's too involved or out of the scope of this meeting. I prefer if we can talk about that later.""

So, you have your meeting, and then you go back to your desk. During your meeting, you always want to take notes. If somebody asks you something really hard, say, "Oh, that's a great question. I'll get back to you on that," and write it down in your notebook. Always have a notebook and a pen ready. You look really important when you're writing. Say, "I'll get back to you on that."

After your meeting, you go back, and if anybody asked you questions you didn't know the answer to, answer those questions via email, and CC the most important people to make sure they know that you followed up on the questions. After your morning meetings, you're going to be hanging around before lunch. If you feel like doing more research, you can read, but during these times, you'll often just be alone, sitting in a cubicle at your desk, doing whatever you choose.

I propose you do research, and if there's anything in that meeting you didn't understand, go look it up. Then you'll go to lunch, and after you come back from lunch, there may be another meeting or two. Meanwhile, if you have a very important meeting right after lunch, you can even, perhaps, skip lunch or just grab it quickly so that you can study the materials necessary so you know what's required for that after lunch meeting.

And so on and so forth. Especially if you're new to SAP and you're just learning, you're going to want to use downtime to study and do everything you can to really learn any information that will be required of you during the meetings.

So, that's the formula I followed. I'm being a little bit lighthearted about this, but that's pretty much what it's like.

Nobody is going to be standing behind you, looking over your shoulder, asking you to perform some complex task. Getting down towards the end of a project or if it's already installed—these can be a bit heated, but they're not going to bring you in right in the ninth inning. You're going to have plenty of time on the job to do the research and call friends.

If you're calling people, if you can ask intelligent questions, it sounds good that you know other people on different projects. I think it's okay to use your network. It's okay and desirable for people to have extended networks that they can call upon to help them with answers. My key thing is it's a pretty low-pressure job. You're not going to be called upon to give split decisions on a moment's notice about very important things.

Generally, you're not going to be called upon to deliver a key technical piece of information or be on the spot for it, but follow up is very important. If you say that you'll look something up, it's important that you do it. I think this differentiates people that will be in this business for the long haul. People that are good and know their stuff versus those that aren't and don't.

I, today, don't know everything, but if somebody asks me a question, I'll try to answer it. If we're working on a problem with the system, I'll generally be able to come up with an answer or say this is not supported in SAP, it's going to be in a different module, meaning SAP doesn't do this, and we really shouldn't be doing this.

Hopefully that puts you a little bit at ease that this is the job, the pace is appropriately relaxed, and nobody's going to jump down your throat for needing some time to get the answers that you need.

Interview Questions Realtime

There are three questions that you will absolutely be asked on your next interview.

The first question is, "Tell me a little bit about what you've been doing."

They're going to expect to hear what you've been working on for the past six months. The answer that you need to give is whatever it is they're looking for. So, if this is an oil and gas position, and they ask you what you've been doing lately, your answer is, "I've been implementing SAP for oil and gas."

It might sound cheesy for you to give that answer, but let me tell you, the more you can hear and learn about the job opening, the more information you can provide to them, so you can tell them that that's exactly what you've been doing. Another thing, I don't care what you've been doing for the last six months. If you want to get the job, you need to tell them that you've been doing exactly what they need done, because that's just how this business works, whether that's right or wrong.

The second question they will ask is something specific about the module relevant to the job you're interviewing for. The question might be, "Tell us about the extended classic mode of SRM and how different it is from the classic mode."

This comes down to finding a good interview question that gives you those technical gotcha questions that they're going to ask. The only other advice I have that can help you prepare for those module-specific questions is to know the business processes that are implemented with the module so you can talk about it in an end-to-end manner.

Even if you don't really understand the question or you don't know the exact answer cold, you can say something like, "Well, after the shopping cart is created and our work flow is kicked off, it goes through the approval process. After a document is fully approved, a purchase requisition is created. After a purchase requisition is created, then a purchase order is sent back in, and that fills in a lot of gaps."

I won't go so far to as to say that fully answers the question, but I've said enough to give them an understanding, make them at least minimally comfortable with what I know.

The third question, which they might not ask directly, is: "Why is this project interesting to you, and why do you want to work on it?"

I think that when interviewers start getting into technical scenarios, they're really asking you about what they want done. It's up to you to express interest in the project. For example, if they start asking you about extended classic with POs on a backend with automated fax, I think you need to say, "This is very interesting. This is one of my favorite projects to do."

Through the interview questions, you might get clues about what exactly they're going to implement. In fact, most interviews actually start out with, "Okay, let me just tell you a little bit about what we're trying to do here. We have several thousand employees that are doing everything manually, and now we want to bring this all to SAP."

"So, we're going to be implementing X, Y, and Z." That third interview question has something to do with whether or not you can do what the company needs done. And indirectly, the question really is, "Are you interested in doing what we need to have done?"

I urge you to try to build a story to somehow weave into your interview, the narrative that you've developed in this interview to convince them that you find this project very interesting. "It fits right into the kinds of things I'm interested in learning and working on."

Going back and reiterating those three questions: the first question is, "What have you been doing lately?" The first answer is, "Well, I've been doing this. This is exactly what I've been doing for the last six months."

Number two is demonstrating technical or functional proficiency. "And this is what I know about this. I know that SRM works in all these wonderful ways, and the configurations this way, the functional that way, and I am interested in doing that in the future." I always talk about interviews in this way: past, present, future. When I'm interviewing prospective employees, that's how I think about it.

These are the three questions that will always be asked on every single interview.

And if they aren't asked – I have to say that as a consultant or an IT professional working in this business, it's up to you put them in, or make sure that you offer that information, because it will help you land a job.

Recruiters

I want to talk a little bit more about recruiters and how you can use them to your advantage. Now, if we take a step back, we have to think about the market for contingent workers in the information technology marketplace. In essence, there are many very, very big companies.

We'll call those employers that have a need for certain things to get done, certain skills. SAP is one example of those skills. And they have a rough idea that they need something done. They don't, however, have any idea how to find the people that possess the appropriate skill sets to get these things done.

Employers need to have some tasks done, and there are people out in the marketplace that are willing to do them. That's us.

Big companies have two choices. They can go after and try to find these people themselves, if they've developed a competency to do so, or they can use brokers. Brokers are the recruitment companies and headhunters. These are the recruiters that I've been talking about. The knowledge that we have to be armed with is that brokers take advantage of this lack of good information in the marketplace.

And I think recruiters are dipping their hands into both pockets, so to speak, since the recruiter has information about employees in the market. The recruiter also has information about the employers in the market, so they're put in the middle here in this special place of trust that they shouldn't necessarily be granted.

They know who the employers are, how much they're willing to pay, and they also know who the employees are and how little they're actually willing to accept in exchange for their work. So, you have these recruiters in the middle that are taking advantage of all this information.

They're out to squeeze you, and many of them have quotas on the percentage of your salary that they must take; otherwise, they'll just find somebody else. Maybe even somebody less qualified. That's what the recruiters do. There still remains the fact that skilled IT people are scarce, and if you work this the right way, you have the opportunity to negotiate once a match is found between you and an employer that needs your skills.

There's a great deal of negotiation to be done. I want to talk about the market forces that play out, and that companies out there rely on these brokers and recruiters for the vast majority of hiring. You have to deal with them.

Recruitment companies are there for a reason, because in many ways, they solve the lack of information for employers.

Many times, you just have to view them as a necessary evil. They're a gatekeeper. There are things that you can do to pull the balance into your favor, and I want this whole series to be about what you can do: information you obtain based on my experiences so that you can start to win and start to take the advantages away from the recruiter.

The very first thing you must do is employ at least five recruiting companies in your next job search. When you send your resume out for a particular job, submit it to as many as possible. Five is a good number. Now, recruiters are going to tell you left and right to only submit once and through their agency.

They're going to ask you to commit to that. They can say whatever they want, but you are in no way obligated to submit only through them. They'll say there's a conflict of interest; they'll say all these things that are just utter rubbish. They'll say, "Oh, it looks bad," for the resume to be sent multiple times to an employer.

That's absolutely incorrect. They want you to go through them exclusively so they can bring this to a client and the client will only be able to hire you through them. Again, that is totally contrary to your mission. Your mission is to get a job. You want to get paid the best price for it, and since it's your labor that's at stake here, you should be in the driver's seat with regard to negotiation.

And let me tell you, if there's an employer and they have one person's resume and they get it from five different companies, who do you think they're going to choose? They're possibly going to go through the recruiter that gives them the best price. Though, price isn't even the most important thing for many companies. They're going to go through the vendor they trust the most. They're going to go through the best vendor, and it's probably going to be the best vendor for you, the best recruiter.

That's one thing that you can do today, right now, that you can change the way you search for jobs and to get the upper hand. Always work with more than one recruitment firm, preferably five, as this will immediately give you the upper hand in negotiation, because you can say, "Well, I've got this offer through many different firms. If you can't come up $10 in rate, this isn't going to work out."

If you've made your way through the interview, they'll be scrambling to give you that extra money because they want to make a deal. The one thing you can do right now to get that leg up is to use no fewer than five recruiters.

Another thing that recruiters do is act as your personal sales network. It would be great if you could arrange all of your contracts directly with end clients, or direct clients as they say, but sales cycles in this business are very long.

It's a relationship-driven business. One of the things about specialization is that certain people are good at some things, and others are good at other things. In many cases, it serves contractors best to let recruiters do the sales piece for them. Recruiters work in a sales-oriented culture, whereas IT people are more like an engineering culture.

One of the great advantages of working with recruiters is you send them your resume, and they, in turn, market you. Good recruiters will do this. Good recruiters will fix your resume. They'll take care of everything. I haven't touched my own resume for the past ten years because I've built relationships with a couple of really good recruiters who put whatever they need to on my resume for each job.

They tailor it, and they get me jobs. I emphasize a lot about the negative aspects of the relationship between the contractor and the recruiter, because I see a lot of people just getting started being taken advantage of by being billed out for $150 and being paid $50 or $60. That's a bit outrageous.

I've had conversations with my recruiters, and I think 25% is the absolute maximum I'm willing to pay. I realize they need to eat too, and it's important that we strike a mutually beneficial relationship. Yet I find that you're taking any more than 25% is excessive.

If you can get them to commit to this, and you tell them, "I will find out what the rate is." If you can find people that are willing to be honest about your rates, the bill rates and not exceeding 25%, I do think that's approaching a level of fairness. You should think about it as, "I give you 25%, but you keep me fully employed." These recruiters need to be working for you and getting you interviews.

If they're not getting you interviews, if they don't have your schedule filled with interviews, they're not doing their job. You need to find more recruiters, and you can find more recruiters by responding to ads on Dice. Although I really believe if you have your profile set up properly, you don't have to lift a finger. Your phone will start ringing off the hook.

And if your phone isn't ringing off the hook, you're doing something wrong with your posting.

I mentioned earlier, use at least five recruiters for purposes of gaining an advantage when negotiating your rate. You need to use recruiters to gain an advantage of reach, because you simply can't be aware of all of the projects that exist.

Not all recruiters have access to all projects. Of course, they'd love to represent you exclusively, but it can't be your responsibility to figure out where you've been submitted. In many cases, they won't even tell you where you're being submitted, and my philosophy is, "That's okay. I don't need to know. I understand this is your trade secret, but I'll find out eventually."

Think of recruiters as your personal sales force, and in return for selling you far and wide and keeping you employed, they get to take a reasonable percentage.

If you can find honest recruiters that will talk to you about what they're billing you for, though many won't, maybe you just won't work with the people who don't. You want to work with people who are straightforward and honest about what they're billing and what their relationship with the client is.

If they freak out, avoid them like the plague. So, get started right now. Send your resume to five recruiters and start building those relationships. Hopefully, you'll find good ones like I have and you'll work with them for a very long time to your mutual benefit.

Recruiters are taking advantage of a situation, but I think you can use them to your advantage. You have to know what's going on in the market, know their purpose, and use them as a sales network for finding work for you.

Resume

First, your resume must have no gaps in work experience. It has to show that you've been fully employed all the way up until this very month, in fact, that you are currently employed.

I don't care if you haven't been working for the past ten years. You need to show that you've been building your skills and that you are, in fact, working right now. You have to show that you're working today. If you're not, they won't look at you.

Say you're working somewhere. Otherwise, I don't know where you'll go. If you say you've been out of work for several years, you will continue to be out of work for several more.

Second, if you're applying for a job in a specific area, such as SAP sales and distribution, you need to show that you've been working in SAP sales and distribution for the past several years.

It's really up to you to decide how much to put on your resume, but if you say on your resume you've been working as a manager at a video game store for the past ten years, you're not going to get the job. Your resume probably isn't even going to go to the client. So, put that you're working today and that you've been working for the past several years doing exactly what it is they need done.

Third, you need a university education. You need to have a U.S. phone number, a U.S. address. You need to have experience that looks like you're taking on more and more responsibility and that you haven't taken any steps backward. Okay, so, you're moving from being on the project team, working out configuration, to team leader. Not, "I was a manager of 60 employees." And then you're moving back to work as a functional consultant.

Your resume has to make sense. You need to include specific examples of things you've worked on, such as, "Implemented a warehouse management system that took care of 10,000 warehouses, shipping, satellite receivers."

I've been consulting at a senior project management level for many years, and recently, my wife and I had our first child. I forgot my own advice, and I sent my resume out to a recruiter, saying I took ten months off, which was true, to have this baby. And guess what? No takers. So learn from my mistake. The first time I forgot my own advice, I paid.

Chapter Five

BW Functional

Let me briefly discuss the differences between BW and Basis.

Basis is the insulation of the underlying components of the SAP software. For example, I install the AB APPS stack, then the ECC 6.0 so that MM and SD can run. Then I install the IT (Internet transaction server), and all the Basis components so that the SAP system, as a whole, can run.

Basis is very important because it keeps the servers running. It handles installs, upgrades, and much of the "heavy lifting" in SAP. That's why there's such strong demand for Basis. Systems like MNSD, SM, and CRM are important because they run transaction processes, and those systems are the business.

That's what the software people use to run the company for taking orders, sending invoices, and making journal entries. I don't want to undervalue the importance of BW, because when people are truly using analytics and not just Excel spreadsheets to run a company, it is a vital piece of software and it needs a corresponding amount of importance.

But, and this is a big but, I've been to dozens of Fortune 500 companies all around the world, and none of them have attached the importance to BW that it needs. As a functional consultant, I've stepped out on a limb many times to explain at length to discuss the importance of analytics. Once they understand what analytics are, they respond, "Oh, this is amazing, this is something we have to have. It's great. Wow, I can't believe we did business before without this."

The sad reality is a lot of the people in BW today aren't good enough. They don't know the software well enough, or they can't communicate about it well enough to enlighten a company about the power and impact of analytics for an operation.

In fact, it's so important to me, that on the very first day of my workshops, I explain what BW does, how they can get data out of the system, and how to use the system to make decisions about the future of their company.

Every time I end up installing a new transaction processing system, the company lets the analytics fall off the table. BW should be a very, very high priority.

You can choose what to study. You can choose how to make investments in your own human capital. As you're making that choice, if you look at the market and you look at how BW behaves, you'll see that yeah, it's a great piece of software, it's important, but companies somehow never quite get there.

If you see that, it just doesn't make sense to make the investment of time and commitment to move into BW as your primary skill set. I think if you're working in MM, SDPM, PP, QM, WM, PS – any one of the core modules that helps a business with their transaction systems, which is part of their core system – you will have a more stable employment situation because companies all have transaction systems.

How companies choose to do reporting is something altogether different. They may use BW or they might use Excel or they might use flat reports. They might use customer reports or business objects. They might use anything. The fact that they might use anything is enough for me to say, "Well, they can choose many different things, so it's not a good enough module for me to invest time in it."

BW is a great skill to pick up in addition to one of the core modules. However, before investing all of your precious time and resources into studying it...be careful. Know that while it is important, oftentimes in big companies it just falls off the table.

Choose Important Modules

A question I'm often asked is: "I understand it's best to choose a module that's important to running a business. Why? Is it because those modules pay more than Basis, or you're seen as more valuable because you're helping to produce revenue instead of being part of a cost center? Or are there fewer people that specialize, so they are more valuable, or is it something else?"

I recommend staying as close to the business as possible, and my exact recommendation is to try to be working on a transaction processing system. If you were studying IT 101, you learn what a TPR is. A Transaction Processing System is an information system required to transact a company's business. When someone calls a company and orders a product, they have to have a system in place to take care of those orders.

Correspondingly, these transaction processing systems are very important to the business, because they can't run without them, and businesses tend to take care of things they can't run without.

An example is a large automotive manufacturing business I consulted for in North America, they made most of their money on selling parts – a business where you have to keep track of hundreds of thousands of different things and where they're located so you can ship customers the right thing when they place an order.

As they were transitioning to SAP, the system went down and they couldn't ship parts. All the executives that were involved in that system going down lost their jobs. Really.

It's best to choose a module that's important to running the business. Why? Because if it's important to the business, you will be important to the business. If you're working on something that they can get rid of without any consequence, then they can get rid of you without any consequence.

I know BW is a hot area a lot of people go after, and BW is important, but companies just aren't that smart about using analytics.

So, if you're comparing MM to BW, there's no comparison. The MM people, the companies need warehousing, materials management, goods receipts. They need that stuff more than they need analytics. You want to work on things that are important to your particular business, because when you're working on something that's important, that makes you important. And it makes your employment much more certain and sustainable.

Working on peripheral technologies, such as something really new, that is not understood to have such a direct impact on the bottom line, that isn't a good idea. Stick to core modules, like MM, SD, FICO, or their add-ons, like CRM and SRM.

Config, Enhance, Modify

You'll hear a lot of terms thrown around during a project, about what you're doing in the system. The most confusing one is customizing/customization.

When I, as a senior functional consultant, say I'm doing my config, I'm doing my customization. So, just like I go to the IMG (implementation guide) and start opening config items, when I make a change, I think even the button says customization.

In the context of how everything should be done in standard SAP, customization doesn't mean you're not doing it in the standard way. It just means you're configuring. And those two terms are many times used interchangeably. Customization is configuration, and that means you're clicking check boxes and radio buttons, and turning things on and off.

I call those customization artifacts. I can say, "I changed this artifact." When you make a change to a switch and then you save it, which represents real work. It's an artifact. It's not programming, where you're typing in lines of third or fourth generation programming language that are then compiled and interpreted. It's not like that, but it's something similar.

It's important to know that customizing is the same thing as configuration. Configuration is standard in SAP. It's normal to do this. A lot of people call these enhancements.

The next level of doing something not in the standard is called an enhancement, formerly called user exits. Now, they're often called a BADI (Business Add In).

An enhancement is not necessarily bad. You're not changing away from the standard. SAP puts these hooks in their code that allow you to jump in and do certain things on your own. Maybe you have fields that need to be checked in a certain way. For example, let's say you're taking your credit card number. You want to check that the first digit is a four for Visa or five for MasterCard, but SAP doesn't do that. So you have a user exit that after the system sees a credit card number, the user exit wakes up, looks at the number, does the check, and lets you know if it sees what it expects to see.

That is a simple enhancement. It is changing the standard, but not in an irretrievable, difficult way. The key distinction there is an SAP upgrade path in their maintenance plan. If you have developments that are registered enhancements for SAP, the software will upgrade automatically. It's not like they'll be wiped out and you'll lose those enhancements, whereas a modification might do that.

If you have some source code, you make a change, and then you upgrade it and it would overwrite that code; and then you'd be left with a problem later on. In SAP, we're talking about systems that are vast in scale. I've worked at places that have had thousands of modifications and changes and it takes a massive effort to keep track of that during upgrades.

The reason that off-the-shelf software saves companies so much money is that it reduces development costs. So customizing and configuration are okay. Developing an enhancement or a BADI or a user exit is sort of one step up. It's okay, but you may receive some pushback. If it addresses a business process or if it helps inefficiency in the business process, there's no reason not to do one, especially if you have a developer around.

Now, that brings us all the way up to the most serious sort of change, a modification. This is something that requires a fundamental change to the SAP source code. This is easy to do, and many times, it's justified.

A really good functional consultant helps a company navigate the political problems surrounding changing the business process. To me, that's what IT, implementing ERP, and software is all about: helping businesses change their processes to be more efficient, to work more smoothly. Many businesses don't even have real processes in place. It's not documented, and this is what you try to do for your clients.

You're helping them implement better business process by using software, and if you can map, you start with the software, understanding all the steps that are required. You can tell them, "In SAP, this is how it is done. Step one, we do this, step two, step three, step four, step five, and here's how the process terminates. This is how we're going to do it now."

The best consultants are able to negotiate and help companies change their processes and fit that square peg into a round hole. You know, actually sculpt that square peg so that it fits into SAP. Much of the time, it's an education for the company. That's why I say: "Consultants, you need to know your software."

It's up to you to show them how it works and so, in the case that they're starting to talk about making enhancement, that's going to be a big deal, because that means somebody couldn't figure out a way to have this business either change the business process, which is what you really should be doing because people can be told to change their style of work, or there's some kind of failure.

If you're doing an enhancement or a modification, something broke down. Either the SAP software was so bad that it didn't fit this business process or the people were so inflexible that they would not change their business process. Many times, that will cause the project manager to raise their eyebrows.

Let's look at SAP and the way the software's working. Let's look at the business process to see how the business is working and why these aren't compatible.

So, those are the three tiers of getting SAP to work. The first one is customizing and configuration, which is standard. The second one is enhancements, BADIs, user exits, which are programming and development. The third is a modification.

If it's standard, but it's work that maybe you should try not to do, and core modifications is something that is possible. It's development, but try to avoid it at all costs, mainly because somebody upstairs will ask, "Well, why are we modifying this system that we've paid so much for? Can't we change the business process?" That's what I would ask.

"Why can't we, what's wrong here? What am I missing? Can't we use this million dollar software? You're telling me that our business is so novel and so unique that we can't map it to the software?" I have a hard time swallowing that, and I've been working in SAP for a long time. So I know that it's possible. You just have to get it done, or you have to be honest. Many times, it comes down to consultants who are questioning enough and who are persuasive enough or can navigate these political waters to ensure they won't step on any toes.

People working in big businesses are working on a small piece of the puzzle, and they get attached to their little piece. So, you can't be too aggressive. You have to make them feel comfortable that you're not pulling away their piece of the little business that they think they own or that they think they're running. Be a little bit sensitive to their fears.

One way to do that is to help them learn SAP and say, "Before, you were in charge of running procurement for this company, and you knew that. Now, you're going to be working in SAP, and this is a good thing because these skills are portable and you can take these anyway and not just work at XYZ Company." So, I covered the three sorts of changes that people are going to be making to SAP, and which ones are good and which ones are bad.

This all definitely fits within the SAP way of doing things, and the better you understand config, enhancements, and modifications, you won't have any big surprises.

Functional vs. Technical

I'm going to take the time to answer some important user questions that I've received. The first one is, "What does functional mean? I understand that programmers and Basis people are technical, but are the business people who use the modules considered functional, or are the functional people the IT people who support and enhance the modules like, HR, FICO, etc.?"

"If I'm a project manager for a SAP installation or upgrade, then am I technical or functional? If I was a business, a warehouse project manager, would I be considered functional or technical?" This is a really good question, because I often talk about the importance of being functional versus technical.

The way to understand or to think about it is that a functional resource or a functional person is working on how the software fulfills a business purpose. For example, in my work as an SRM consultant, I'm a functional consultant. I'm teaching my clients how to best use SAP software to match their business processes.

Functional people are like business analysts. They're consultants, project team members that possibly work for the client. These are people who are necessarily just users of the software.

Saying that you're functional implies that there's some sort of consulting role involved or power user, and if you say, "I'm an SAP functional consultant," to certain people, that means something very specific. It means you know how to configure the software.

Now, a functional person definitely knows how to use the software and it also implies that they know how to configure. So, are functional people the IT people who support and enhance the modules like HR and FICO? Yes. That is another good way to characterize what functional people do. If you're a project manager, that means you're the ultimate functional person. You're the boss of the functional people. Project managers mostly rise through the ranks of functional consultants.

Technical means programming, whether that's markup in HTML, or ABAP, or Java, or WD AB APP objects. In all these technologies, programming means technical. People in the SAP role work on interfaces like ALE, EDI, ALE, XI, PI.

Now, the last question is about BW.

"If I were a BW project manager, would I be considered functional or technical?" If you are a project manager on a BW project, you're functional, because you're explaining to the business at a high level how analytics fit into their organization and how important it is to have a working analytics package. And a BW may be a more technically-oriented module by virtue of how it's modified, maintained, and implemented in organizations.

Yet, I think it's a mistake to think about BW as technical. In projects where I'm a team leader or project manager, I say BW is the way that you get data out of SAP, and your business should be run on data. And if it's not being run by the numbers, then there is a problem. So BW, in my mind, should be functional, but it's looked on in many places as technical work, but that's a mistake.

So, to recap. You can think of functional consultants as people who are business analysts or who configure the software. And you can think of technical people as those who are programmers. I recommended that if you want to be successful in information technology as a broad career choice, and specifically in SAP, that it's important to transition your skills to a more functional skill set. I also recommend that for a few reasons. The first one is that software is getting better, and there's less of a need for programmers.

There is still a need for technical consultants, and if you're a technical worker, and you're happy being a programmer, great. You need to know that the market forces are driving technical work away because it's expensive, and there will be a reduced need for programmers and technical developers as software improves. There is now a tendency in business to shift development expenses to less expensive places in the world.

You can take advantage of this, but you have to understand where you live. So, if you're in a developing nation where there is a lot of work or a lot of need for technical resources, then fantastic. If not, you need to transition your skills to a functional area where you can interface more closely to the business. I have prepared a sheet that quickly describes the future of employment information technology.

One of the things you'll see is that I believe there's a shift to functional work rather than technical. Many people in IT think it's the end of the world or they'll have to find a new career. I don't think that's the case. You just have to be aware of the basic changes in the marketplace and know how to adapt to them.

Functional is business analysis, and technical is programming. There are some gray areas, BW being a notable one, but know the functional people are closer to the actual business process and working with clients. Another way to think about it is: technical people work for functional people.

The SAP Way

I want to talk a little bit about the SAP way, and while it might sound kind of strange at first, the more you learn about SAP and the people who work in SAP as consultants and managers and employees, you'll find that there's a certain way they do things and it's not very democratic.

You can use this to your advantage when you start to learn, and certainly when you're talking to people on interviews. When you start working, there's an SAP way to do things, and then there's another way to do things, such as a third-party way. You might think if you start working in MM and the BW doesn't work very well and you need some kind of a report on the system, then you need to develop a custom report to get the information you want.

While that is a very good and reasonable idea, it would be met by resistance in the SAP team. They'll say, "Hold on a second. We don't need a third-party tool. We need to use SAP to do this. We can use SAP tools, an existing report, an existing screen." That is the SAP way. You use the standard system. You don't develop anything new and you don't use a third-party tool. You don't do a customization or enhancement or a modification.

It's important for me to talk about this SAP way and using the standard, because this is one of the promises that ERP is supposed to deliver: return on investment, savings of cost in development, and maintenance. Part of the way that you obtain this advantage is by sticking to the standard.

By using a COTS package like SAP, you don't have to develop anything and maintenance is taken care of by the software provider. If you look at the history of IT and big software system, this is somewhat of a revolution. In the beginning, every system was one-off.

If you were a programmer in the '70s, into the '80s, you were the one person who knew this system, and you could count on being employed, maybe even maintaining a single system. Yet, software's gotten a lot better. If you think about it, software, in general, has been around for less than 50 years. The business is starting to mature. So, COTS is one answer to that, and SAP is a real world solution implemented by very big businesses.

Everywhere you go, people will say, "We use standard SAP. We don't do developments, we don't change the standard." Many companies will want to, and depending on the company you go to, they'll have different ideas about business and adapting their business process to work with SAP. You can identify the really good companies by if they're willing to change their business processes to adapt to the software.

I find the best companies are very interested in changing their processes, making it better and adapting to SAP, because they know that overall, it is less expensive to change their process than it is to change SAP. Meanwhile, if you're working at a company and they're changing SAP left and right, from a contractor's perspective, you just hit the jackpot because you'll probably be there for five years.

I want to talk about the culture of the SAP way, and how to navigate that. There's a phenomenon where people say, "Well, let's use the standard SAP process. We're not going to do any customization. We're not to do any modification."

Something you're going to repeat over and over, and nobody can disagree with about, is: "This is supported in the standard. It's standard SAP. It's best business practice. Let's do it this way." Those are the magic words. Once you say that, nobody should argue with you. If they do, maybe they'll say, "Oh, that's not in the standard," or "That's going to require a modification or enhancement." If somebody stands up and says that, you can respond, "Oh, okay, well, let's make sure that's in the standard."

You want them to use SAP standard, and that applies to configuration, AB APP programs, to everything. Very few times, you're going to actually be asked to make a change to the SAP. Certain things must be changed, like smart forms. Those don't count as customizations or modifications or enhancements.

To summarize, things are done the SAP way and recommending something else will be a big surprise to other people. Even if you're offering a sensible solution, such as a third-party reporting tool, the response will be, "Where were you coming from?" Everything is done inside SAP in the SAP system, from creating users to reporting. All the transactions you process. If you're just getting started, it's important to know that there are no alternate solutions. If you're working in SAP, that's all you implement.

There are many, many third-party connectors that have APIs going into SAP. SAP people know those connectors are unnecessary and that everything can be done in SAP.

What is Configuration

I received the following question: "What does "configure" in SAP mean? Is it choosing settings from among these offered, or is it more complicated than that? Can you give some examples?" Configuration in SAP is one of those activities that a functional consultant tends to take on.

Although technical people might do this, too, I think configuration is a process of going through the IMG, and I'll tell you a little more about that in a minute.

Configuration involves selecting check boxes, radio buttons, typing in short values of two or three characters, etc. For example, one of the things you talk about in the area of procurement is unit of measure. Unit of measure is ounces, inches, centimeters, grams, kilograms.

Currency is an easy thing to think about, too – dollars, pounds, rupee, so they'll understand what a lac is. So, let's say I want to configure and add a new unit of measure, like a google, maybe I'm a molecular scientist and I need to come up with a new unit of measure because I invented a way of keeping track of atoms or molecules, and I could have a google of molecules.

Somebody who was configuring that in an SAP system would add that unit of measure, and they would say goog is one google. Generally, when I say configuration, I mean making settings in SAP that are not program-related changes. It's anything but programming, including adding notes to the organizational plan, adding units of measure, check boxes, and radio buttons. Configuration is done in SAP via transaction SPRO.

The vast majority of your configurations will start there. That's called the implementation plan or the IMG. You'll have access to this if you're a "Breaking Into SAP" student. Go on the SAP access link, and you will log into a live SAP system, and you can start configuring this

SAP system by typing in transaction SPRO, looking in this IMG by expanding the items there, and then looking at the settings. That is the active configuration, and that comprises the majority of what a SAP functional consultant actually does.

Functional consulting is the process of talking to a company about their business processes and helping map that company's business process to what SAP is capable of, and that is accomplished via configuration. So, if I talk to a company about how they procure goods and services, the first thing we have is a purchase requisition, then a purchase order, then the purchase order is sent to the customer, they send the goods, and we do goods receipt. Then we send the customer an invoice, then they pay, they send us an invoice, and we pay them. That's a pretty standard purchasing process.

So, the functional consultant is saying, "I have to make sure that purchase requisitions are configured appropriately." Then you go to SAP, go through the configuration, the purchasing configuration, and then you try the purchase requisition transaction. The same goes for purchase orders and invoicing. Invoicing is interesting because it may be cross-functional. You have people in the finance department that care about how invoices are applied, which accounts they're posted to, and so on and so forth.

Configuration is the act of making changes in SAP. Everything in SAP can be saved. If you click a radio button and you save that, it's a configuration artifact and can be transported in the future.

It's important to know that in productive SAP environments, you have a quite rigorous change management system implementing. You do your changes, you play in the sandbox, you do your development on the development server, and once you're done, it's called transporting from development to test or production. The important thing to know is that configuration is a real artifact.

It's very important to your career in SAP.

What is Functional

I have another student question. "What does functional mean? I understand that programmers and Basis people are technical, but are the business people who use the modules considered functional, or are functional people the IT people who support and enhance the modules, like HR or FICO, etc.? If I'm a project manager for an SAP installation or upgrade, then am I technical or functional? If I were a BW PM, would I be considered functional or technical?'" These are terms that people working in SAP use to talk about themselves.

If I say I'm SAP functional, I'm a consultant. I'm somebody who's configuring the solution. I'm a power user inside of an organization. I think you've got it when you say people who support and enhance the modules, like HR, FICO, etc., yes.

It's good to think about the project manager as the chief functional person on a project, and that they understand the systems and how everything fits together. It's rare that you would see a project manager that's strictly technical. A BW project manager might be the one exception to the rule if you had a Basis project to have a technical project manager. Even then, it would have to be so rare, because project managers need to understand the context the systems happen in and how they touch other modules. So I would say even a BW project manager would be functional. Functional people, in fact, support, configure and enhance the modules where technical people in SAP are more writing programs and keeping the basis set up.

PART II: CONCEPTUAL QUESTIONS

Question 1: *MRP Procedures in MM-CBP*

What MRP procedures are available in MM-CBP (Consumption Based Planning)?

A: Various material planning methods are used in MRP (Material Requirements Planning) including:

Reorder point procedure (VM)

Forecast-based planning (VV)

Time-Phased materials planning (PD)

These are specified in material creation (MM01) under the MRP 1 tab.

Question 2: *Planned Order Creation*

Under what conditions are "planned orders" created? What may planned orders be converted to and how is that conversion accomplished?

A: Planned orders are always created when the system creates an internal procurement proposal. In the case of vendor procurement, the MRP controller may create a planned order or directly create a PR. The next step for a planned order is to be converted to a PR so it goes to purchasing and is to eventually become a PO. A planned order can be converted to a PR using transaction code MD14.

Question 3: *Organizational Levels of Enterprise Structure in R/3*

What are the organizational levels of the Enterprise Structure in R/3?

A: The top level of the organizational plan is the client, followed by company code, which represents a unit with its own accounting, balance, P&L, and possibly identity (subsidiary). The next level down is plant, an operational unit within a company (HQ, assembly plant, call center, etc.). The purchasing organization is the legally responsibly group for external transactions. This group is further subdivided into purchasing groups.

Question 4: *Organizing Purchasing Organizations*

What are the different ways to organize purchasing organizations?

A: A purchasing organization may be responsible for multiple plants and this is referred to as "distributed purchasing." On the other hand, "centralized purchasing" features one purchasing organization per plant.

A purchasing organization doesn't necessarily need to be assigned to a company code. This would enable procurement for every company code as long as buyers are acting for an individual plant, and that plant is assigned to the purchasing organization. Hence, a plant may be assigned to more than one purchasing organization.

Question 5: *Special Stocks*

What are "special stocks"?

A: Special stocks are stocks that are accounted for but are not owned by the client, or are not stored at a regular facility. Consignment, sales order, and project stock are examples.

Question 6: *Transferring Materials Options*

What are some of the options available to transfer materials from one plant to another?

A: Although it is possible to transfer materials from one plant to another without a stock transport order (STO), many advantages are lost including entering a vendor number, planning a goods receipt in the receiving plant, monitoring process from PO history, and the ability to create STO directly from a MRP PR.

Question 7: *Stock Transport Order Movement Types*

What are some of the common stock transport order movement types?

A: One step transfers of materials can be posted using MT 301. Other various transport scenarios differ in the MTs by the goods issues and good receipts. Common goods issues may use MTs 303, 351, 641, or 643 in the STO. An STO's good receipt often uses MT 101.

Question 8: *Purchase Order vs. Purchase Requisition*

What is the difference between a purchase order and a purchase requisition?

A: A purchase requisition is a document type that gives notification of a need for materials or services. A purchase order is a document type that is a formal request for materials or services from an outside vendor or plant. Procurement types may be defined at the line item and can be standard, subcontracting, consignment, stock transfer, or an external service.

Question 9: *"Indirectly Created" Purchase Requisition*

What is an "indirectly created" purchase requisition?

A: An indirectly created purchase requisition has been initiated by CBP, the PS project system, PM maintenance, and service management, or PP production planning and control. The "directly created" purchase requisition, on the other hand, is created by a person manually in the requesting department specifying materials / services, units, and a delivery date.

Question 10: **RFQ and Quotation Form**

What is an RFQ and how is it different from the quotation form?

A: An RFQ is a purchasing document and an invitation to a vender(s) for quotation regarding needed materials or services. If multiple RFQs are sent to multiple vendors, the system can automatically determine the best quote and send rejection letters in response to all others. The RFQ and the quotation form are one in the same in the system, as vendor's quotes are entered directly in the RFQ.

Question 11: **Transactions Leading to Change of Stock**

What are the transactions that will result in a change of stock?

A: A goods receipt is a posting acknowledging the arrival of materials from a vendor or production, which results in an increase in warehouse stock, a goods issue which results in a reduction in stock, or a stock transfer moving materials from one location to another.

Question 12: *Posting Goods Movements Via Shipping Application*

When would it be prudent to post goods movements via the shipping application?

A: Picking, packing, and transportation operations need to be planned in detail. Also, in shipping, you can manage movements like returns from customers and vendors as well as returns to stock. Movement types in shipping start with a 6.

Question 13: *Reservation*

What is a reservation?

A: A reservation is a document used to make sure that the warehouse keeps a certain amount of a material or materials ready for transfer at a later date. It contains information on what, quantity, when, where from and to. Reservations help effective procurement by utilizing the MRP system to avoid out of / lack of stock situations.

Question 14: *Generating Purchase Requisition*

Can you manually generate a purchase requisition referencing a purchase order or a scheduling agreement?

A: A purchase requisition cannot be created with reference to either of these, as they are documents controlled by the purchasing organizations.

Requirements can be automatically generated with MRP that reference a scheduling agreement if the source list is maintained for item-vendor combination.

Question 15: *GR/IR Account's Relation to Inventory*

How is GR/IR account related to inventory?

A: If you are involved with inventory, then you need the GR/IR account (inventory account) when the IR is posted. If you are not involved with inventory, then the system does not need the GR/IR account when the IR is posted; the system needs a G/L instead of the GR/IR account.

Question 16: *Planned and Unplanned Consumption*

How do planned and unplanned consumption affect movement types?

A: In a customized movement type, you have defined which consumption value gets posted in the movement. Many will always be planned or unplanned, but for some there is a dependency if the movement references a reservation. This would be planned consumption.

Question 17: *Departmental Views*

What are departmental views?

A: All functional areas of the system use the same material master data. The material master data is defined in individual screens (departmental views) that can be added as needed. Thus, a material can be created with only basic data, and other departments can add other information later as it becomes available.

Question 18: *Validity of Material Data*

Is material data valid for all organizational levels?

A: Control of master data depends largely on whether a company sets up its organizational levels as centralized or decentralized. Some material data is valid for all organizational levels while other data is valid only at certain levels (i.e., client, plant, sales organization, etc.).

Question 19: *Physical Inventory Sheets for Inventory Cycle-Counts*

Why would you want to create physical inventory sheets to perform an inventory cycle-count on a material or materials?

A: For a cycle counting procedure, physical inventory documents need to be created. These are used to record inventory levels of the material being cycle counted.

Use transaction MICN. Click on the Execute button. On screen "Batch Input: Create Physical Inventory Documents for Cycle Counting," perform the following: click on the Generate Session button and click on the Process Session button. This procedure details how to create the physical inventory documents for cycle counting in a batch, rather than one at a time, based on certain criteria. This would print physical inventory documents for all material / batches that meet those requirements.

Question 20: *Blanket Purchase Order vs. Framework Order*

What is the difference between a blanket purchase order and the framework order?

A: In general, the blanket POs are used for consumable materials such as office paper with a short text, with item category B. There need not be a corresponding master record, for the simplicity of the procurement. The FO, framework order, document type is used. Here, the PO validity period as well as the limits are to be mentioned.

The GR, or service entry for the PO, are not necessary in the case of blanket POs. One need not mention the account assignment category during creation of the PO. It can be U, or unknown, and be changed at the time of IR.

Question 21: *Release Procedure*

What is release procedure?

A: Release procedure is approving certain documents like PRs or POs by criteria defined in the configuration. It is sensible to define separate release procedures for different groups of materials for which different departments are responsible, and to define separate procedures for investment goods and consumption goods.

Question 22: *Releasing PO Item by Item with Multi-Line-Item PO*

If you have a multi-line-item PO, can you release the PO item by item?

A: No, a PO is released at the header level meaning a total release or "with classification."

PRs, on the other hand, have two release procedures possible. "With classification," as described above, and "without classification," where it is only possible to release the PR item by item.

Question 23: *Material Type*

What is a material type?

A: A material type describes the characteristics of a material that are important in regards to accounting and inventory management. A material is assigned a type when you create the material master record. "Raw materials," "finished products," and "semi-finished products" are examples. In the standard MM module, the material type of ROH denotes an externally procured material, and FERT indicates that the relevant material is produced in-house.

Question 24: *Price Comparison*

What is a price comparison?

A: Perform a price comparison using ME49 and one may compare quotations from different vendors.

Question 25: *Source List*

What is a source list?

A: The source list identifies preferred sources of supply for certain materials. If it's been maintained, it will ID both the source of supply and the time period. The source list facilitates gaining a fixed source of supply, blocked source of supply, and / or helps us to select the proffered source during the source determination process.

Question 26: *Steps from Material Creation Through Invoice*

What are the various "steps" in the MM Cycle from material creation through invoice?

A: The following creates a rough picture of the MM Cycle. Create material, create vendor, assign material to vendor, procure raw material through PR, locate vendor for certain material, processing GR, goods issue, and invoice verification.

Question 27: *Information Relating to Material's Warehousing*

Give some examples of the information relating to a material's storage / warehousing.

A: Some examples are unit of issue, storage conditions, packaging dimensions, gross weight, volume, and hazardous materials number. Also, there are various storage strategies information and options.

Question 28: *Consignment Stock Features*

What are the various features of consignment stocks?

A: Consignment stocks remain the legal property of the vendor until the organization withdraws the material from the consignment stores. The invoice can be due at set periods of time, for example monthly, and it is also a configuration possibility that the organization will take ownership of the stock after a certain period of time. Consignment stock is allocated to the available stock because the consignment stock is managed under the same material number as your company's stock.

The most important characteristic of consignment stock is that it isn't valuated. When the material is withdrawn, it is valuated at the price of the respective vendor. Before procuring the stock, consideration should be given if one consignment is coming from multiple vendors. If so, we can manage all of them independently at the price of the individual vendors. In the info record, we will maintain three different prices for the same material for three different vendors.

Question 29: *Quotation*

What is a quotation?

A: Once a vendor has received an RFQ, the vendor will send back a quote that will be legally binding for a certain period of time. Specifically, a quotation is an offer by a vendor to a purchasing organization regarding the supply of material(s) or performance of service(s) subject to specified conditions. The quotation then needs to be maintained in the "Maintain Quotation: XXXX" screens.

Question 30: *Source List*

What is the source list?

A: The source list identifies preferred sources of supply for certain materials. If the source list has been properly maintained, it will identify both the source of a material and the period of time in which you can order the material from the source.

Question 31: *Invoice Verification*

What is an invoice verification?

A: The invoice verification component completes the material procurement process and allows credit memos to be processed. Invoice verification includes entering invoices and credit memos that have been received, checking accuracy of invoices with respect to price and arithmetic, and checking block invoices (these are the ones which differ too much from the original PO).

Question 32: *Types of Invoice Verification*

What are the different types of Invoice Verification?

A: **Invoices based on purchase orders.** With purchase-order-based invoice verification, all of the items of a purchase order can be settled together, regardless of whether or not an item has been received in several partial deliveries. All of the deliveries are totaled and posted as one item.

Invoices based on goods receipts. With goods-receipt-based invoice verification, each individual goods receipt is invoiced separately.

Invoices without an order reference. When there is no reference to a PO, it is possible to post the transaction directly to a material account, a G/L account, or an asset account.

You can park invoices that reference POs and GRs as well as invoices with no reference in the system. When you park a document or change a parked document, neither substitution nor validation is supported. The system only carries out these functions after you actually post a parked document.

Question 33: *Reasons for Allowing Negative Stocks*

Why would an organization need to allow negative stocks?

A: Negative stocks are necessary when goods issues are entered necessarily (business process reasons) prior to the corresponding goods receipts and the material is already located physically in the warehouse.

PART III: CONFIGURATION RELATED QUESTIONS

Question 34: *Creating Movement Type*

How do you create a movement type? When will movement type numbers be odd?

A: When prompted by a dialog box after an activity, you copy a movement type. Select the field "Movement Type" and "Continue." In the "Define Work" area, enter the movement type to be copied in "From:" and the name your new movement type in the "To:" field. Now choose "Continue." Choose the desired movement type you want, then choose Edit → Copy as and re-type the selected movement type with the new type copy in all dependent entries and make sure to begin with a proper prefix (9,X,Z). All control indicators are copied to the new movement type. Review the new movement type and change any necessary controls. Reversal movement types are numbered as the number type plus one. For example, the reversal for movement type 451 (returns from customer) is 452. As a last step before saving your settings, add a copy the reversal movement type and enter it in "Reversal / follow-on movement types."

Question 35: *Message Determination Facility in MM-PUR*

How do you adopt standard settings for the message determination facility In MM-PUR?

A: The message determination facility is by default active, and message determination schema is supplied for all purchasing documents including POs, PRs, RFQs, etc.

All of the desired message types must be maintained. Choose Master data → Messages → Purchasing document → Create or Change from the Purchasing menu. Add the message type and pick the key combination. The key combination decides the condition table where the condition record is stored. Enter all needed items. On the next screen, create the individual condition records. Using the menu options Goto → Means of Communication, enter the proper peripheral, or output for each message record. Save.

Question 36: *Setting Price Control for Receipts*

How do you set price control for receipts (goods / invoice) telling the system how to value stocks?

A: Transaction code OMW1 allows you to set price control to S (standard price) or V (moving average price).

Under standard price (S), the materials and accounting documents are both valid. The one with the lower value will be posted with a price variance entry.

Question 37: *Accessing the Materials Management Configuration Menu*

How do you access the materials management configuration menu?

A: Transaction code OLMS has a host of options that are not accessible through the IMG.

Question 38: *Accessing MM Configuration Transactions*

How are the various MM configuration transactions accessed?

A: Transaction codes OLMD accesses MM-CBP, OLMB accesses MM-IM, OLME accesses MM-PUR, OLML accesses MM-warehouse management, OLMS accesses material master data, and OLMW is the proper transaction for valuation and account assignment.

Question 39: *Materials Management Tables*

What are some of the more important materials management tables?

A: EINA contains general data of the (purchasing) information record; EINE includes purchasing organization of the same. MAKT is the materials description table, MARA-general materials data, MARC-plant data for materials, MARD-storage location data for material, MAST-material to BOM link, MBEW-material valuation, and MKPF-header material document.

Some of the tables that directly pertain to the document types are T156 movement type and T023/T024 groups material and purchasing.

Question 40: *Custom Fields in Pos and RFQs*

Can you add custom fields to POs and RFQs?

A: Yes. You must add custom fields to the customer including structures I_EKKODB and I_EKPODB.

Create a project via CMOD for enhancement MM06E005. Follow the documentation for MM06E005, and create the sub-screens for function group XM06 using transaction SE80. Add fields to the appropriate screen. It is recommended that you call the screen fields EKPO_CI-name or EKKO_CI-name. This simplifies transferring data to / from the screen. Put code in EXIT_SAPMM06E_018 to transfer data from sub-screen to structure E_CI_EKPO. Put code in EXIT_SAPMM06E_016 to transfer data from database to sub-screen using structure I_CI_EKPO. In the PBO of the sub-screen, do any processing to make fields display only, or hide them. If you need values from the main screen to make decisions in the sub-screen, define variables in the global data part of the function module, and fill the variables in EXIT_SAPMM06E_016 (PBO of main screen). Make sure everything has been activated like user exists, screens, etc.

Question 41: Converting Planned Orders into Requisitions in MRP

Where can you dictate how planned orders are converted into requisitions in MRP?

A: Look at the transaction code OPPR indicator. Assign proper indicator.

Question 42: Updating / Creating Material Master Records

What SAP program is used to update or create material master records?

A: RMDATIND is used to update material master records and can be used for such assignments as extending all materials to a new plant.

Question 43: Views Possible for Material

What views are possible for a material?

A: The material type selected controls the views possible for material.

For a material to be used in the system, it needs to be created for each plant. Multiple views of a material are possible, but at a minimum, the material needs to have a description and a base unit of measure assigned on the basic data view. Additional department views (i.e. accounting, sales, purchasing, MRP, warehouse) can be added at a later time by extending the material. As additional plants are added, a material will need to be extended to the plants before it can be used there.

Question 44: *Production Resource / Tool as Material*

When can a production resource / tool be defined as a material?

A: A production resource / tool can be defined as a material if purchasing and inventory functions are to be carried out for that PRT.

The information required to be input is dependent upon which department views are being created. Thus, material master information is typically entered at different times by numerous system users. Note that to add a view, the "Create Material" transaction is used rather than the "Change Material" transaction.

Question 45: **Creating New Material**

When creating a new material, what may prompt some of the possible material types?

A: Pressing F4 gives a list of choices. Select the material type for the material you are creating. For example, FHMI for prod. resources / tools, ROH for raw materials, FERT for finished products, etc.

Question 46: **Adding Views of a Material**

How do you determine which views of a material need to be added or to see which plants a material has been extended to?

A: You can use transaction MM50.

Extending a material to a different plant requires selecting the new plant on the organizational level screen. Note that all views of a material are not extended unless they were selected on the initial screen. In addition, each plant may have a different system configuration requiring additional inputs on each of the departmental screens. Material changes made in one plant do not change that material in other plants.

Question 47: *Setting User Defaults for Views and Organizational Levels*

How can you set user defaults for views and organizational levels?

A: The user defaults for views can be set under Menus: Defaults → Views. Select those views to be checked on by default when generating a new material. Select "view selection only on request" when the select view pop-up is to be by-passed unless selected.

For organizational levels, Menus: Defaults → organizational levels. Enter those organizational levels to be defaulted when generating a new material. Select "org. Levels / profiles only on request" when the select view pop-up is to be by-passed unless selected.

Question 48: *Automatically Copying Material Type from One View to Another*

What needs to be present in order for material type to be automatically copied from one view to another?

A: When creating any view, the industry sector and material type will be automatically copied from an existing view, so long as at least one view exists.

Question 49: *Notifying Supplier / Internet Personnel of Invoice Plan Settlement*

How do you create a document/e-mail notifying your supplier or internal personnel when an invoice plan is settled?

A: The IMG setting is Material Management → Logistics Invoice Verification → Message Determination.

If these settings are not made, the message "Invoicing Plan: No Message Was Found for Partner XXX, Company Code XXX" will be given. If the notifying documents are not required, simply turn off the message by changing the message from "error" to "information" using Material Management → Logistic Invoice Verification → Define Attributes of System Messages.

Question 50: *Preventing Using from Using Standard MM Movement Types*

How can one keep users from using standard MM movement types?

A: Standard movement types should not be deleted from the system. The account assignments, however, may be deleted for a particular movement type in table T030 using transaction OBYC.

Another way to achieve the same result is to enter movement type in transaction OMJJ. Remove MBXX from allowed transactions.

Question 51: *Release Procedure for PRs and Pos*

How do you define a release procedure for PRs and POs?

A: Use transaction ME54 and ME28 respectively.

Question 52: *Change Characteristic*

How do you change characteristic?

A: Use transaction code CT04. Follow these steps: format (numeric, character, etc.), unit of measure, templates, required entry, intervals as values (?), descriptions for texts for characteristics and characteristic values, display options for characteristics on the value assignment screen, allowed values, default values that are set automatically on the value assignment screen.

Question 53: *Class Creation*

How do you create a class?

A: Class is defined as the group of characteristics, which can be attributed to a product. Use transaction CL01. Enter the value for the class name and a small description. Select the group from it. The values on the different tabs are not mandatory, so you can skip the values if you wish or you can go to any extent needed. Save, and the class is created.

Question 54: **Configuring Release Procedure**

How do you configure the release procedure?

A: Use transaction OMGQ.

Question 55: **ROH and FERT**

Will ROH have a sales view? Will FERT have a purchasing view?

A: They shouldn't because ROH-type materials are procured from the outside, not sold, and FERT-type materials are created inside and aren't procured.

In some special cases, we have to sell raw materials (ROH) and buy finished goods (FERT) from outside sources. The views must be extended in these cases using transactions OMS2 and MM50.

Question 56: **Creating Vendor Account Groups**

Where do we create vendor account groups, or screen layout in vendor master?

A: Using SPRO, Financial Accounting → Accounts Payable/Receivable → Vendor Accounts → Master Records → Preparations for Creating Vendor Master Records → Define Account Groups With Screen Layout (Vendors) or Define Screen Layout Per Activity.

Question 57: **Key Fields for Material Master**

What are the key fields for the material master?

A: Material Groups, External Material Groups, Divisions, Material Status, Labs & Offices, Basic Materials, Storage Conditions, Temperature Conditions, Container Requirements, and Units or Measure Groups.

Question 58: **Main Purchasing Tables**

What are the main purchasing tables?

A: EKBN   Purchase Requisition

    EBKN   Purchase Requisition Account Assignment

    EKAB   Release Documentation

    EKBE   History of Purchase Document

Question 59: **Creating a Material**

How do you create a material?

A: Use transaction code MM01. Name the material, choose an industry sector, choose a material type, create or copy the views, add a basic description, give its attributes / values, MRP information, reorder point, accounting valuation, warehouse management information, and then save the data.

Question 60: *Data Points Provided by Purchasing*

What are some of the data points provided by purchasing for a material?

A: Some of the key inputs when creating a material are base unit of measure, purchasing group, reminder days, tolerance levels, shipping instructions, GR processing time, JIT schedule indicator, critical part (?), etc.

Question 61: *Lot Size Attributes*

What are the lot size attributes a material can posses?

A: Lot sizing dictates the reorder quantity for a material. A material can have a static, periodic, optimum, or fixed lot size.

Question 62: *Vendor Creation*

How do you create a vendor?

A: Use transaction code XK01. Add the vendor name, company code, purchasing organization, account group, and the vendor address. Next add the country, bank key,bank account, account holder (an actual name), and then save the data.

Question 63: *Material Assignment to Vendors*

How are materials assigned to vendors?

A: Information record links materials to the vendor, thus facilitating the process of selecting quotations. Use transaction code ME11 or Logistics → Material Management → Purchasing and then Master Data → Info Record → Create.

Question 64: *Information Record Data*

What data does the information record contain?

A: The information records has data on units of measure, vendor price changes after a certain level, what materials have been procured by a specific vendor, price and conditions for relevant purchase organization, tolerance limits for over / under delivery, vendor evaluation data, planned delivery time, and availability time the vendor can supply the material.

Question 65: *Creating Information Record*

How do you create the information record based on the material master record?

A: In the IMG, Master Data → Info Record → Create. Enter vendor number, material number, purchasing organization or plant number. Enter the number of the information record if external number assignments are used (left blank, the system will assign a number). Enter the general data for the vendor, order unit, origin data, and supply option, customs tariff number. Next, enter the vendor's planned delivery time (used for scheduling), responsible purchasing group, and standard PO quantity (used in conjunction with price scales for price determination). Check the control data. The tolerance data and the responsible purchasing group are taken as default values from the material master record. Enter the net price. Now, from the top of the screen Go To → Texts to display the text overview. You can enter the info memo or the PO text. If the PO text is already defined in the material master record, it appears as a default value. Save the record.

Question 66: Configuration Steps for Purchase Requisitions

What are some of the initial configuration steps for Purchase Requisitions?

A: Define Document Types, Processing Time, Release Procedure (with and without classification), Setup Authorization Check for G/L Accounts, Define Number Range.

Question 67: Reasons for Setting Up Stock Transport Order

In initial configuration, why would you have to set up stock transport order?

A: If it is required to carry out an inter-plant stock transfer through SD, then this configuration is required and must be carried out.

Question 68: Configuration Steps for Inventory Management

What are some of the initial configuration steps for inventory management?

A: Plant Parameters, Define System Message Attributes, Number Assignment (allocate document type FI to transactions), Goods Issues, Transfer Postings, Define Screen Layout, Maintain Copy Rules for Reference

Documents, Setup Dynamic Availability Check, Allow Negative Stocks (?).

Question 69: *Configuration Steps for Physical Inventory*

What are some of the initial configuration steps for physical inventory?

A: Define Default Values for Physical Inventory Document, Batch Input Reports, Tolerances for Physical Inventory Differences, and Inventory Sampling. Cycle counting should be configured as well.

PART IV: PRACTICAL / TROUBLESHOOTING RELATED QUESTIONS

Question 70: **Processing Vendor Returns without PO Reference**

How can you process vendor returns without a purchase order reference?

A: Use transaction code ME21N.

Look for the return columns and click it at the item details, MIGO_GR , goods receipt for return purchase order. Movement type will be 161 to deduct the stock and 162 for reversal. Before saving, check if there is a check in the return column to ensure that it is a return purchase order.

Question 71: **Invoice Verification**

How can an invoice be verified?

A: Transaction code OLMR may be utilized.

Question 72: **Changing Standard Price in Material Master**

How do you change the standard price in the material master?

A: The standard price in the material master can't be updated in a direct manner. A great way to update it is to fill the fields Future Price MBEW-ZKPRS and the Effective Date MBEW-ZKDAT for the material on the accounting view. Next, go to Logistics → Materials Management →

Valuation → Valuation Price Determination → Future Price → Activate. TCODE MR2B, program RMMR2100. Lastly, run the BDC that was created to update the standard price.

Question 73: **Goods Receipt**

How do you perform a goods receipt?

A: Use transaction MIGO. Enter the header data, select the movement type, enter the PO number, select the PO items to be copied, and then post the document.

Question 74: **Posting a Goods Receipt without PO Number**

How can you post a goods receipt if the PO number is not known?

A: If you selected PO Number Not Known in transaction MIGO, you can specify search criteria for the POs on the initial screen. The system then displays a list of purchase orders. Select and copy the required PO items.

Question 75: **Displaying System Reservations**

How do you display a list of all reservations in the system?

A: Run report *RM07RESL*.

Question 76: **Movement Type Error**

If you have created a custom movement type and you get a "not allowed" error, where should you first look for the cause?

A: Using transaction code OMJJ, check "Allowed Transactions" for the customized movement types.

Question 77: **Finding Stock Item Logical Value**

How do you find the logical value for stock item by date?

A: Use transaction MC49.

Question 78: **Disabling Reservation in MRP**

How can you disable a reservation in MRP?

A: Use transaction code OPPI to check "block stock."

Question 79: **Adding Attachments to Purchase Order**

How do you add an attachment to a purchase order?

A: One may attach any document to a PO manually without using the document management system in SAP, but no attachments can be added while you create a PO using ME21N.

Save your PO and then open the PO using ME22N. There you can attach a document with the Service for Object button. Click the Service Object button → Create → Create Attachment, then select your window directory, the file to be attached. This attachment is only for internal information. The system will not print this document automatically along with a PO printout.

Question 80: *Generating Automatic PO*

How do you generate an automatic PO after creating a PR using a particular material?

A: In MMR and VMR, check Auto PO (MM02/XK02).

Maintain the source list and select the indicator for the source list record as MRP relevant (ME01). If more than one source list record is generated, make one of them fixed. Run MRP, and the PRs generated will be pre-assigned with the source of supply (MD01). Enter ME59 for automatically creating POs from PRs.

Question 81: *Header and Item Level Data in PO*

Where is the header level and item level data saved in a PO?

A: In SE11, we can see this information in table EKKO and EKP0 respectively.

Question 82: **Material Master Data**

Where is material master data saved?

A: Tables MARA and MARC.

Question 83: **Issuing a PO**

How do we know if a PO has been issued?

A: Bring the requisition up by using Material Management → Purchasing → Purchase Requisition → Display. Where the requisition overview screen is displayed, select an item by clicking on the selection box to the left of the item. Click on the General Statistics icon on the application tool bar. Select item. The screen appears, in the middle, under Order Statistics, in the field Purchase Order;, if there is no number, the PO has not been issued.

Question 84: **PR with Master Record vs. PR without Master Record**

What is the difference between a PR with a master record and without a master record for the material being ordered?

A: If the master record exists, then all of the information about the source list, information record, and vendor evaluation already exist in the system. If we don't have a master record for the material we are ordering, the material is generally being ordered for direct usage or consumption. You can specify which consumption account is to be charged which is also known as account assignment. For example, we assign the purchase costs associated with a requisition to our sales order or cost center.

If the first situation exists, many times purchasing enters into a longer-term purchasing agreement with a vendor, which is called an "Outline Agreement." If the outline agreement is done, then purchasing cannot issue a purchase order against a PR. It can only set up such an agreement (either a "Contract" or a "Scheduling Agreement").

Question 85: *Altering Purchase Requisitions*

Can you change a purchase requisition after it has been created?

A: Yes. Use transaction ME52N. Check to see if the PR has already had a PO issued against it. If so, you must inform the purchasing group. Check if the PR has been approved. If so, you may only make changes to a limited extent and may be subject of approval. Check if the PR was created by MRP. In this case, you don't have much control over the modification process.

All changes to items are logged and stored. Information stored includes when the information was changed, who changed it, what the changes were, etc. Select the desired item in the item overview and choose Go To → Statistics → Changes.

Question 86: *Creating Consignment Stocks*

How do we create consignment stocks?

A: Everything is the same as a normal PR or PO, except: Enter the item category "K" for the consignment item. This ensures that the goods receipt is posted to the consignment stores and an invoice receipt cannot be generated for the item. Also, do not enter a net price.

Question 87: *Vendor Evaluation*

What is vendor evaluation and how do you maintain it?

A: Vendor evaluation helps you select the source of supply by a score assigned to a particular vendor. The scores are on a scale of 1 to 100 and are based on differing criteria. Use transaction ME61 and enter the purchasing organization and vendor number.

Question 88: *Master Data Components Detailing Company Procurement*

What are the components of the master data that details a company's procurement, used by vendor evaluation, for example?

A: The key components of master data are: Info Record (ME11), Source List (ME01), Quota Arrangement (MEQ1), Vendor (MK01), Vendor Evaluation (ME61), and Condition Type (MEKA).

Question 89: *List of Vendors*

How do we get a proper list of vendors to send an RFQ?

A: Either use the information record to see who has sold a particular material to the organization in the past, or go through the source list.

Question 90: *Source List Creation*

How do you create a source list?

A: Use transaction ME01. Enter the material number and the plant data. Enter source list records, validity period, period of time material is procurable, vendor number, responsible purchasing organization (or number of the agreement or contract), PPL (if the material can be procured from another plant), fixed source (?), MRP control.

Also, a check should be done to see whether any source list records overlap. To do so, choose Source List → Check.

Question 91: *Returning Items to Vendor*

How will items be returned to the vendor?

A: When you are posting a goods receipt for a PO, you can also enter items that you want to return to the vendor. To do this, you no longer have to reference the purchase order with which the goods were originally delivered. From the item overview, choose 161 (return for PO) as the default value for the movement type. Enter the data for the return item(s) and post the document.

Question 92: *Performing a Goods Issue*

Where do you perform a goods issue?

A: Use transaction MIGO.

It is possible that when MIGO is accessed, a different document screen appears than the one required. This occurs because SAP remembers the last goods movement transaction accessed per user login. To reach the goods issue purchase order screen, click the dropdown icon in the transaction field and select "Goods Issue."

Question 93: *Performing a Goods Issue, Part II*

How do you perform a goods issue?

A: Use transaction MIGO. On the initial screen, enter the header data (you need not enter the movement type or the plant as these are automatically copied from the order). Choose Goods Issue → Create with Reference → To Order... If you know the order number, enter it directly. Using the by-products indicator, you can simultaneously post the goods receipt of planned by-products. Using the choose transaction / events indicator, you can display all transactions / events for an order and choose the transaction / events for which you want to post a goods issue. Copy the desired item(s). Check data on the overview screen. Post the document.

Question 94: *Performing an Invoice Verification*

How do you perform an invoice verification?

A: If the invoice refers to an existing document (PO, etc.), then the system pulls up all of the relevant information like vendor, material, quantity, terms of delivery, payment terms, etc. When the invoice is entered, the system will find the relevant account. Automatic posting for sales tax, cash discount, corrections, etc. When the invoice is posted, certain data such as average price of material and price history are updated. Use transaction MIRO.

Question 95: *Displaying Parked Documents*

How do you display parked documents?

A: There are two possible transactions to use here. They are FB03 and FBV3. The first shows all posted document types. This is the best choice if you think the document has been posted to you actual balance. The later shows only parked documents that have not yet posted to your expenditure balance. These documents are still encumbrances. It is the best choice if you are trying to find which documents are still awaiting completion or approval.

This transaction is very similar to the FBV2 transaction used with P-Card reconciliation and marking parked documents complete.

Question 96: *W, V, and F Fields in FBV3*

What do the W, V, and F fields show about the status of a document in FBV3?

A: An X under the W column means the document is subject to workflow. Most documents on this screen should have an X in this column. However, not all documents are subject to workflow (cash deposits, etc.). An X in the V column means that the document has been marked as complete. If they are subject to workflow, they have been sent to workflow for approval when they were marked complete. An X in the F column means that the document has been approved and posted to expenditures. This column will always be empty in this screen.

An X under W, but no X under V means that you have not marked the document as complete. If it hasn't been marked as complete, use FBV2 to check the document and, if it is correct, mark it as complete. You can quickly go to the document from the list screen by double clicking on the document number. When the document is displayed, click on document on the menu bar, and then click on change in the drop down menu. The transaction will switch from FBV3-Display to FBV2-Change. An X under both W and V will mean it is waiting for approval and you may need to check the approval path to see if has met with a delay.

Question 97: *Transaction MRKO Error*

If you are using transaction MRKO, vendor settlement, and we get an error message (FS217 or M8443 etc.), how would you go about troubleshooting this?

A: To troubleshoot this problem, we have these steps to follow. Set up output condition type "KONS." The output type specifies the kind of output to be produced. The output type is predefined for your area of the R/3 system. If alternative choices are possible, you can, of course, list them by pressing F4. The output type can specify, for example, a printed form that you need for internal use or a form that you want to send to a customer or vendor (for example, an order confirmation). The output type can also be an internal electronic mail message that you want to send to staff in another department. To create an output type, we use transaction V/30. Click on New Entries; go to where you can define a new output type (i.e. KONS). Once you have fed all of the data in the screen, you can save it, and we will have a new output type.

Now, use transaction MRM1, where we will maintain conditions for the output type KONS. When you press the key combination tab, you go to the "Create Condition Records (Consignment): Fast Entry" screen. Here you define the company code, partner, etc. Hit the save button. Now you have conditions associated with the output type KONS.

Now, we must maintain the appropriate tax code in the information record. Use transaction ME12. Be sure info category is consignment. Hit <Enter> and you will go to the screen "Purch. Org. data 1." Hit <Enter> again and you will go to the next screen, where you need to maintain the tax codes. Put in tax code "I0," which means exempt. The next step would be to go to the G/L account and update the "Tax Category" using transaction FS00. "Drop down" the box for tax category and you will get some options. Choose the first option "Only Input Tax Allowed." Hit save. Next, go to check the "Field Status Compatibility at G/L Account"; use transaction SE38. Now, enter the program number "RM07CUFA" and hit "Execute." Now enter movement type "291 K," which is used for the goods issue related to consignment. When you press the execute button, you will see screen "Field Selection Comparison: Movement Type – G/L Account." Now, check the compatibilities of all the fields; if a particular field is not compatible, then there will be an error message with a red highlight. Now the signs plus, minus and dot denote whether the entry in that particular field is "Required," "Optional" or "Suppressed," etc.

Now, the error could be because of the following reasons: If the mvt column has a "+" and account column has a "-"; If the mvt column has a "-" and the account column has a "+". Once you fix the value, you can go to the error log and see if there are any more errors there. The last step would be to run transaction MRKO. Now, you get all of the "Not Settled," "Pending Transactions," or good receipts recently done. Then, go to the previous screen and press the "Settle" tab and execute it again for settling the documents. Now the transaction goes through and the vendors are paid automatically. If after doing this, we still get the error message, then we could also go to transaction OMRM and change the error message to a warning message. The other place to find the error messages is transaction SE31.

Index

INDEX

Index

Index

Index

www.ingramcontent.com/pod-product-compliance
Lightning Source LLC
Chambersburg PA
CBHW031548080326
40690CB00054B/663